IVAN III

and the

Unification of Russia

is one of the volumes
in the
TEACH YOURSELF HISTORY
LIBRARY

Teach Yourself History

VOLUMES READY OR IN PREPARATION

IVAN III

and the

Unification of Russia

by
IAN GREY

THE ENGLISH UNIVERSITIES PRESS LTD
102 Newgate Street
LONDON E.C.1

FOR
KATE

First Printed 1964

Copyright
Ian Grey, 1964

PRINTED AND BOUND IN ENGLAND FOR
THE ENGLISH UNIVERSITIES PRESS LTD, BY
HAZELL WATSON AND VINEY LTD, AYLESBURY, BUCKS

A General Introduction to the Series

THIS series has been undertaken in the conviction that there can be no subject of study more important than history. Great as have been the conquests of natural science in our time—such that many think of ours as a scientific age *par excellence*—it is even more urgent and necessary that advances should be made in the social sciences, if we are to gain control of the forces of nature loosed upon us. The bed out of which all the social sciences spring is history; there they find, in greater or lesser degree, subject matter and material, verification or contradiction.

There is no end to what we can learn from history, if only we would, for it is conterminous with life. Its special field is the life of man in society, and at every point we can learn vicariously from the experience of others before us in history.

To take one point only—the understanding of politics : how can we hope to understand the world of affairs around us if we do not know how it came to be what it is? How to understand Germany or Soviet Russia, or the United States—or ourselves, without knowing something of their history?

There is no subject that is more useful, or indeed indispensable.

Some evidence of the growing awareness of this may be seen in the immense increase in the interest of the reading public in history, and the much larger place the subject has come to take in education in our time.

This series has been planned to meet the needs and demands of a very wide public and of education—they are indeed the same. I am convinced that a most congenial, as well as a concrete and practical, approach to history is the biographical, through lives of the great men whose actions have been so much part of history, and whose careers in turn have been moulded and formed by events.

The key idea of this series, and what distinguishes it from any other that has appeared, is the intention by way of a biography of a great man to open up a significant historical theme; for example, Cromwell and the Puritan Revolution, or Lenin and the Russian Revolution.

My hope is, in the end, as the series fills out and completes itself, by a sufficient number of biographies to cover whole periods and subjects in that way. To give you the history of the United States, for example, the British Commonwealth or France, or Russia *via* a number of biographies of their leading historical figures.

That should be something new, as well as convenient and practical, in education.

I need hardly say that I believe in people with good academic standards writing once more for the general reading public, and of the public being given the best that the universities can provide. From this point of view this series is intended to bring the university into the homes of the people.

A. L. ROWSE

ALL SOULS COLLEGE,
        OXFORD.

Preface

IN the period from the mid-15th to the second half of the 16th century, as the result of a long process, constantly checked by calamities, the people of Great Russia finally achieved unity and the Russian nation came to birth. The movement towards unity and nationhood had suddenly gained momentum in the 15th century when the Grand Princes of Moscow emerged as the leaders and Moscow was established as the centre and capital of Russia. Even as it was forming, however, the new nation was continually endangered by the aggression of its neighbours—Tatars in the south and east, Lithuanians, Swedes, and Germans in the west and north-west. The fact that it survived and gathered strength was in part due to the sturdy endurance of its people and in part to the leadership of its rulers. Grand Princes Ivan III and Vasily III and Tsar Ivan IV, the Terrible, were all men of outstanding ability and vision, but Ivan III was the chief architect of Russian unity in these crucial years.

This period is, in fact, of great importance in the study of Russia's history. The rise of Moscow, the leadership of its rulers and the princely opposition to them, serfdom, and other basic factors, which influenced and even dominated events in subsequent decades, have their roots in these years. Despite this importance, however, Western students have had to rely almost entirely on short chapters in general histories for accounts of these developments.

This study is intended as a contribution towards filling the gap in the material available in English. It seeks to recount briefly and clearly the main events in Ivan III's reign, leading to the unification of Great Russia under Moscow's rule. The story is complex and at times confused. The Renaissance and the growth of the independent nations of Western Europe at this time were confined within a comparatively small area, and were, moreover, well documented. The struggles of the Russians towards nationhood took place in the immensity of the Eurasian plain and involved the peoples of Asia as well as of Europe. Moreover the complexity is aggravated by paucity of documentation. There are many gaps in our information about the men and events of the period, which I have indicated in the text. Soviet historians have carried out important research in this early chapter of Russian history, and have clarified some of the issues, but many problems remain.

The Notes for Further Reading set out the main sources on which I have relied, and which are available for further study. I would like nevertheless to express my indebtedness to the works of Solovyev, Klyuchevsky, and Professor G. Vernadsky on which I have drawn heavily.

IAN GREY

Contents

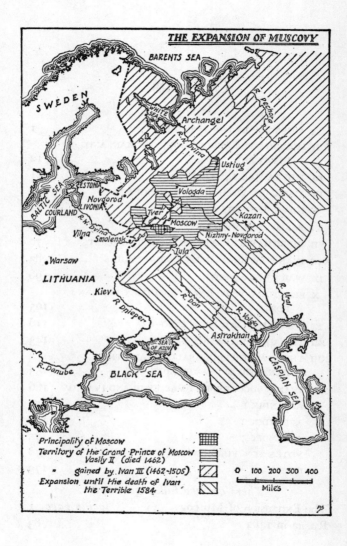

THE EXPANSION OF MUSCOVY

BARENTS SEA

SWEDEN

WHITE SEA

Archangel

R. Pechora

Ustiug

BALTIC SEA

ESTONIA

Novgorod

LIVONIA

COURLAND R.W. Dvina

Vilna

Smolensk

Vologda

Tver

Moscow

Kazan

Nizhny-Novgorod

Warsaw

LITHUANIA

Kiev

R. Dnieper

Tula

R. Don

R. Volga

Astrakhan

R. Ural

SEA OF AZOV

R. Danube

BLACK SEA

CASPIAN SEA

Principality of Moscow
Territory of the Grand Prince of Moscow
       Vasily II (died 1462)
   "   gained by Ivan III (1462-1505)
Expansion until the death of Ivan
the Terrible 1584

0   100 200 300 400
Miles

Chapter One

Muscovy in the 15th Century

THE movement of the Russian people towards unity and nationhood can be traced with some certainty from the 8th century. The Eastern Slavs then inhabited the lands lying between the Black and the Baltic Seas and the Don and the lower Danube Rivers. They were especially concentrated along the banks of the upper and middle reaches of the Dnieper River, which provided the main artery of trade with Byzantium and the Arab world. Here they hunted, worked the soil, and traded with furs, wax and honey. But, split into rival groups and settlements and exposed to constant attacks by nomad enemies, they lived a hazardous existence.

Defence was their most important need and one which became more urgent as the pressure of predatory attacks mounted. For this reason they turned in the 9th century to the Varangians for help and leadership. The Varangians or Norsemen were adventurers and traders from Scandinavia, who had come south for trade and plunder and with ambitions to dominate the route from the Baltic to the Black Sea. According to the early chronicles, the Varangian leader, Rurik, made Novgorod his headquarters about the middle of the 9th century. Then in 878 Oleg, his successor, moved southwards and established Kiev as his capital. He gathered the Eastern Slavs into a loose federation, known as Kievan Russia, which marked the beginning of the Russian nation. [See Appendix 1.] During these years the people became organized into city-states, each with a prince who headed his own retinue of warriors and was responsible for the defence of the city and its trade. Political life was centred on these trading towns, and commerce was the dominant factor of their economic lives.

In the 10th and 11th centuries Kievan Russia reached its greatest extent and power. Moreover, in the reign of Grand Prince Vladimir [978–1015] the Russians adopted Eastern Christianity as their faith. Vladimir had embraced Orthodoxy both on religious and on political grounds. He considered that, together with the example of Byzantine autocracy and the prestige of his marriage with the sister of Emperor Basil II, the church would help secure the hegemony of Kiev and of the dynasty of Rurik. It would also foster closer trading relations with Byzantium.

The conversion of Vladimir and, by his order, of the Russian people to the Christianity of the Eastern Church was one of the most momentous events in Russian history. The Orthodox faith, although imposed, was to sink deep roots among the Russians, permeating their lives and helping to shape their history, their culture, and their national character.

In the reign of Vladimir and then of Grand Prince Yaroslav [1019–54], Kiev grew into a large and splendid city, advanced beyond many other European cities in civilization at the time and renowned as a centre of trade. Byzantine influence was strong. The Grand Princes sought to make their capital an imperial city like Constantinople, and Yaroslav engaged Greek builders to erect the cathedral of St Sofia and other fine buildings. A library and theological college were attached to the cathedral. Many monasteries were founded and the Monastery of the Caves, the most renowned of them all, fostered a rich spiritual and cultural tradition which was to endure. The ruling house of Rurik received recognition from the royal families of Christendom, and considerable inter-marriage took place between them. But the glory of Kiev was transient.

The power of the Grand Princes was not sufficient to prevent constant feuding among the Russian princes and at times a princely anarchy reigned. The death of the ruling prince was frequently followed by family struggles for the throne of Kiev. The feudal order which the princes had developed, the overriding importance of commerce, and the advent of Christianity all combined to prevent the development of a sense of nationhood among them. While the power and prestige of their Grand Princes increased, the union of the Eastern Slavs began to disintegrate. Even for purposes of common defence they could not put aside their rivalries. After the break-up of the Khazar empire and the failure of the great plan of the Kievan Prince, Svyatoslav, to re-establish the union of the forest and steppelands, and thus to dominate trade from the Baltic to the Black and Caspian Seas, Kiev was constantly challenged by nomads. The Pechenegs, the Kumans, and other Turkish tribes attacked in waves. Furthermore in the 12th century the Germans began driving eastwards, pushing the Lithuanians and Letts before them. The Russians were then faced with Lithuanian pressure in the north, while still defending themselves against the nomads in the south and engaged in internecine struggles.

Gradually the Russians drifted away from their allegiance to Kiev and moved northwards. Many found their way into Galicia and into White Russia, or Belorussia, which were to pass into the hands of Lithuania–Poland at a later date. The most important stream of migration was to the north and north-east, to the regions of the upper Volga and its tributaries, and from this stream Muscovy and the Russian empire were created.

This movement to the north marked the beginnings of a new stage in the political and economic development of the Russians. They remained split into groups, but based no longer on the trading towns. They were divided now among the independent principalities and ruled by their princes. Trade remained important, but it was no longer the basis of their economic life. Agriculture took its place, as they began to clear areas of forest, and the free peasant labour worked the land. This stage in their development, lasting from the 13th to the mid-15th centuries, was to be followed by the unification of the Russians under the central authority of the Grand Princes of Moscow.

Of the principalities which formed in the upper Volga region in the 12th century, Vladimir-Suzdal claimed to be the successor of Kiev and was at first the most powerful. In 1169 its prince, Andrei Bogolyubsky, even led a daring raid on Kiev and captured the city. The prestige and authority of Kiev were never to recover from this attack. Some seventy years later the Mongols razed Kiev to the ground and conquered the Russian lands. [See Appendix 2.]

The Mongol invasion of the 13th century, the last great westward movement of the Eurasian nomads, was one of the most shattering and fateful events in history. From causes which no one can divine the hitherto insignificant Mongol tribes, numbering less than a million in population, suddenly stirred with furious aggressive energy. The leader of genius who welded these Mongol tribes together was Temuchin, more usually known as Genghis or Chingiz Khan [1167–1227], who sought to conquer the world. His wild horsemen first came into conflict with the Russians in 1224, when they crossed the Volga and defeated the Kumans and the southern Russian princes on the Kalka River. Under Chingiz Khan's successor the Mongol army, commanded by Baty, his grandson, and by Subatai, the foremost Mongol general, set out to make more enduring conquests. In December 1238 the Mongols captured Ryazan. The principality of Vladimir-Suzdal was next to fall. Other towns, like Pereyaslavl and Moscow, were razed to the ground by the advancing horde, but it stopped short at Novgorod. The dense forests and extensive morasses in what was an exceptionally rainy summer made Baty turn back. Novgorod was thus spared the devastation that other Russian towns suffered, but the Novgorodtsi, realizing that this was merely a respite, were quick to swear allegiance to the Khan.

In 1240 Baty moved westwards again. He took and destroyed Kiev. He then sent part of his army through Poland, while Subatai led the other part across the Carpathians, laying waste Hungary and Croatia. At this time, however, news came of the death of Khan Ogodai and the vacancy of the Grand Khanate. Baty at once withdrew to take part in the Kuriltai, the assembly of Mongol princes, to elect a new Khan. He did not renew his conquest of Europe. Poland and Hungary were left to recover. But Russia remained under the Mongol yoke and from Saray on the lower Volga, which he made the headquarters of the Khanate of Kipchak, or the Golden Horde, Baty and his successors were to exercise suzerainty over the Russians for more than two centuries.

The Mongols did not annex the lands, interfere in local politics, except when they touched on the interests of the Horde, or seek to impose any policy of tatarization on their vassals. Their interests were solely to exact tribute and levy recruits to serve in their armies, and the resulting economic burden and drain on manpower were the most serious effects of the occupation.

From the mid-14th century the Mongol grip on Russia began to weaken, mainly as a result of the dissensions within the Horde itself. By then, too, the Russians had recovered from the shock and terror of the Mongol invasions and from the slaughter and devastation which had for a time brought the national life to a standstill. They were quick to take advantage of the declining authority of the Khans and began to assert their independence.

At this time, however, the Grand Principality of Lithuania emerged as a major power. Her great military leader, Gedimin the Conqueror [1316–41], seized much of west and south-west Russia, including Kiev and most of the Ukraine. Olgerd [1345–77], his son and successor, added further to Lithuanian power by defeating Novgorod, subduing Pskov, and extending his empire to the shores of the Black Sea. Later in the century [1385] Lithuania and Poland agreed a treaty of union and Jagiello, Grand Prince of Lithuania, married the Polish Queen and was himself declared King of Poland. A century and a half later, in 1539, this union was converted into a complete political union, creating the powerful Lithuanian–Polish state.

The growth of Moscow from an insignificant town into the matrix and capital of a new nation forms one of the most fascinating chapters in Russian history. Destroyed by the Mongols in 1238, Moscow began to rise soon afterwards, and it remains a perplexing question why Moscow, and not one of her wealthier and stronger neighbours, such as Tver, Ryazan, or Novgorod, should have seized the hegemony and become the unifier of Russia. Several factors undoubtedly contributed to this development, but the unaccountable accidents of history, which can be recorded, but never fully explained, also played their part.

One of the main factors in Moscow's rise was her geographical position at the centre of the river and land communications of Russia. The town stood on the banks of the Moskva River, which connected the upper Volga with the middle and upper Oka River and, by way of their tributaries and convenient portages, with other mighty rivers like the Don. This position at the very centre of the vast system of waterways was one of the greatest advantages enjoyed by the town. Moreover, this inner position gave Moscow greater security from attacks by Tatars and other enemies, with the result that people of all ranks, especially from Eastern Russia, made their way to the Moscow region for refuge, and this colonizing movement brought a much needed and extremely valuable increase in population.

Another important factor in the rise of Moscow was the ability of its rulers. The early princes do not emerge as individuals, and historians have not agreed about their ability or their importance. Klyuchevsky dismissed them as men of indifferent competence who were favoured by the accidents of history. But all were men who displayed certain common characteristics which make their achievement in developing their town and principality more readily understandable. They were all careful stewards of their estates, enterprising, and tenacious, ruthless and level-headed in the pursuit of their policies.

Ivan I, called Kalita or Money-Bag [1328–41] was scrupulously subservient to the Golden Horde and for his reward he obtained the Khan's consent to the revival of the Grand Principality of Moscow and to the removal of the Metropolitan, the head of the Russian church, from Vladimir to Moscow which thus became the ecclesiastical centre. Moreover, he obtained appointment as collector of tribute on behalf of the Khan, a function which gave him ample opportunity to further the interests of Moscow. Each of these three factors was to prove of decisive importance in Moscow's growing ascendancy, and none more than the new close connexion with the church.

During the Tatar domination the Orthodox church had flourished. The Khans had shown a leaning towards Christianity so strong that at one time Rome had entertained hopes of their conversion. Even after they had adopted Islam they continued to show favour to the Orthodox church, which they protected by charter and whose lands they exempted from all interference and payment of taxes. Under this protection the church grew wealthy; its lands attracted peasants; its churches and monasteries multiplied. A wave of religious fervour moved monks to establish monasteries in the surrounding forests and even in the tundra in the far north. At the same time the church increased the sense of unity and fostered hopes of independence among the subject Russians, and it gave the Grand Princes of Moscow powerful support in their policy of casting off the infidel yoke and of uniting all Orthodox Russians under their rule.

By the middle of the 15th century, however, Moscow's ascendancy had still not been established. The Tatar yoke had virtually been discarded, but Moscow was surrounded by enemies, and the Russian people remained divided, many of them being under foreign rule. The Smolensk region in the west, embracing present-day Belorussia or White Russia, and most of the Ukraine, formed part of Lithuania. Eastern Galicia had been annexed by Poland, and Carpatho-Russia was in the possession of Hungary. The steppelands, starting from Ryazan and Tula and stretching to the

Black and Caspian Seas, formed a kind of no-man's-land, but dominated by the Tatars of the Crimea and the lower Volga, who effectively prevented Russian attempts to settle and cultivate this fertile expanse.

Illustrating this division of the Russian people, the distinct languages of the people had by this time clearly formed. The three tongues were Russian [Great Russian], Ukrainian [Little Russian], and Belorussian [White Russian]. But Church Slavonic remained the common language of each of these divisions, and it was to provide the basis of their literary language. It was, however, more significant that the people all called themselves Russians and their land Russia, irrespective of whether they were under Lithuanian, Polish, or Muscovite rule. This was an important indication of the basic unity of race, religion, and language which all felt and which aided the Grand Princes of Moscow in their policy of unifying the whole Russian land.

In East and West Russia at this time three clear trends were noteworthy in the development of the government and administration. In Lithuania, especially after the first union with Poland, the *pany* or nobles, the equivalent of the boyars in Muscovy, wielded considerable authority. In Poland, whose example infected Lithuania increasingly in the 15th and subsequent centuries, the magnates or great nobles and the provincial gentry, assembled in the diet or *seym*, controlled the budget and exercised even wider restraints on the authority of the king.

By contrast in Muscovy power was being concentrated more and more in the hands of the Grand Prince. Princes and boyars, subject to a few rebellious exceptions, recognized his authority as overriding. The Boyar Council assisted him in ruling, but its powers were ill-defined and it never sought to exercise the restraints which the Polish *seym* or the Lithuanian council of nobles exercised over their rulers. The third form of government was developed in the city-states of Novgorod, Pskov, and Vyatka, in which the *veche*, broadly representative of the citizens, exercised the power.

The magnates, nobles, and boyars formed only a small proportion of the population, the great majority of whom in East and West Russia were peasants. Inhabiting the forest zone in Muscovy, only part of which had been cleared and was fertile, they lived by hunting, fishing, and various crafts as well as by tilling the soil. Of the total population some 95 per cent. belonged to this category, for the Mongol invasion which had destroyed the towns, except Novgorod, and had greatly reduced the importance of trading, had led to an increase in the rural population. The merchant class in Muscovy at this time was small, but it possessed greater wealth and importance in Novgorod and Pskov, while in Poland and Lithuania the merchant class, comprising both merchants and artisans, was more influential.

At the time of Ivan III's accession to the throne in 1462 the position of the Russian lands was still complex and parlous. Muscovy was surrounded by enemies and extensive regions, inhabited by Orthodox Russians, lay still in the possession of Lithuania. Furthermore, the principalities of East Russia were not yet all united under the rule of Moscow. Four principalities—Yaroslavl, Ryazan, Rostov, and Tver—remained independent. More seriously, the city-state of Novgorod with its vast empire stretching across northern Russia, and the smaller states of Pskov and Vyatka, the other free cities, remained outside the authority of Moscow. Finally, Ivan knew that his own kinsmen posed an active threat to his throne and to the stability of Muscovy.

The obstacles and problems thus facing Ivan III were formidable, but so, too, was the growing momentum of the movement among the Russians towards unity. In part, this was a reflection of their need to band together to defend themselves against their enemies and to protect and develop trade. In part, too, the Russian people were feeling their way towards nationhood. At this crucial juncture in their history, they had in Ivan III a ruler who was remarkable both in his ability and his vision.

Chapter Two

Ivan III: The Succession, the Man and his Policy

IVAN III, sometimes called "the Great", was born on 22 January 1440, the first son of Grand Prince Vasily II of Moscow and his wife, Maria Yaroslavna. From earliest childhood he was to find that his father was insecure on the throne and that the principality was wracked by savage struggles which at times recall some of the cruelest scenes in *King Lear*.

Vasily II had succeeded to the throne of Moscow in 1425 at the age of ten. But his uncle, Prince Yury of Zvenigorod and Galich, had strongly contested his right to rule. Anticipating such family rivalry, his father, Vasily I, had even entrusted his widow and sons to the protection of Vitovt, the powerful Grand Prince of Lithuania. But Vitovt had regarded this trust as an opportunity to extend Lithuanian power. In 1430, however, he died and Lithuania encroached no further on Muscovite territory.

In 1433 Yury had defeated his nephew in battle and had assumed the title of Grand Prince. The boyars and people of Muscovy, nevertheless, persisted in regarding Vasily as their rightful ruler and in the face of their opposition Yury finally abandoned the throne and retired to Galich. But he was incapable of remaining quietly in retirement. At Galich he formed an alliance with his three sons, Vasily Kosoy, Dmitri

Shemyaka, and Dmitri Krasny, and mustered a strong army with which in 1434 he again decisively defeated his nephew. Within a few months, however, Yury died and his son, Vasily Kosoy, seized power. But he enjoyed even less support among the Muscovites than his father. Vasily displaced him without difficulty and, to make sure that he did not again become a threat, had him blinded.

The struggle for power was still not at an end. On the death of Vasily Kosoy, his brother, Dmitri Shemyaka, began contending for the throne. He managed to win the support of many Muscovite boyars and also of the Grand Prince of Tver and the Prince of Mozhaisk by alleging that Vasily, after his defeat and capture by the Tatars of Kazan in 1445, had agreed to surrender Moscow to the Khan. Vasily was apparently unaware of these allegations and of the opposition against him aroused by Dmitri Shemyaka. In February 1446 he set out with his two sons, Ivan and Yury, on a pilgrimage to the Troitsa monastery and in his absence Dmitri entered Moscow and seized the throne. He then sent Prince Ivan of Mozhaisk to arrest and strike out the eyes of Vasily, who was afterwards led off to exile in Uglich.

Dmitri was, however, uneasy on the throne of Moscow, particularly as in his plans he had overlooked the young Princes Ivan and Yury. They had been taken by faithful retainers to Murom on the Oka River, where the Ryapolovosky family, strong supporters of Vasily, gave them their protection. Learning where they were hidden, Dmitri did not dare to have them killed, but he used guile. Her persuaded Iona, Bishop of Ryazan, to take the boys into his care, promising him the Metropolitanate as a reward. The Ryapolovsky were deceived by the Bishop's assurances and handed the two boys over to him, whereupon they were seized by Dmitri's men and imprisoned in Uglich with their parents.

Dmitri now knew even less peace in Moscow. His perfidious treatment of the young Princes had increased the opposition among the boyars and people to his rule. Evidently he suffered a crisis of conscience, for he rode to Uglich and confessed his guilt in usurping the throne, but his conscience did not trouble him too severely, for at the same time he exacted from Vasily an oath, recognizing him as Grand Prince. Subsequently Vasily obtained a release from his oath by the abbot of the Kirill-Beloozero monastery. He then gathered his supporters and, marching on Moscow, compelled Dmitri to surrender the throne to him as the rightful Grand Prince.

Vasily II, although now blind, reigned for fifteen years after his restoration in 1447, and during these years his son, Ivan, was constantly at his side. It gave Ivan valuable training in the arts of war and government. He took part in the final campaign in 1452 in which Dmitri Shemyaka was crushed, and in campaigns against the Tatars. At the age of twelve he was married to Princess Maria of Tver, and his first son, also named Ivan, was born six years later. As early as 1449 his father had proclaimed him Grand Prince and co-ruler to ensure his succession and on Vasily II's death in March 1462 he had at once ascended the throne.

In his will Vasily II had followed the Muscovite practice of establishing one son as his chief heir and successor to the title and authority of the principality, while granting apanage principalities to the other sons. To Ivan he bequeathed the title to the grand principality of Moscow, together with one third of the city's revenues, fifteen of the chief towns in the principality, and the city-state of Vyatka which Vasily II had, in fact, brought under his rule in 1459. To Ivan's four brothers and his mother were bequeathed lands and towns, which, while far less than the inheritance of Ivan, nevertheless gave each brother a considerable degree of independence. His mother had only a life interest and her property reverted to her sons in equal proportions after her death. No provision was made, however, for the disposal of the property of a prince who died intestate or without heir. Ivan was to take advantage of this lack of testamentary directive to add to his possessions.

The practice of the Grand Princes of Moscow of bequeathing the major portion of the principality to a chosen son had been an important factor in the rise of Moscow. Other principalities had been fragmented, because their princes had carefully observed the custom of providing roughly equivalent independent princedoms for the sons of each generation. By the mid-15th century many princely families had been so impoverished that the sons of such families had found themselves compelled to seek service in Moscow.

Ivan had thus inherited the title, authority, and wealth establishing him as the Grand Prince and sovereign of Muscovy. But the danger that his position might be challenged by his brothers was everpresent. Vasily II had suffered from savage family rivalries for the throne and he may well have wished to protect his son from similar insecurity which could only endanger the principality and might even result in his son being dethroned. But he did not feel able to resist the force of tradition, which required that each male member of the family should have an independent apanage in which he ruled without interference. Within his principality the apanage prince ruled supreme; he owed obedience to his Grand Prince only in matters arising outside his principality. Such semi-independence was, of course, bound to give rise to struggles for the supreme power.

In his testament Vasily II had exhorted his sons to "respect and obey your elder brother, Ivan, in my place". In the past similar exhortations had not proved effective in preventing attacks on the position of the senior brother. In fact, the succession to the throne was constantly embittered by feuds. Ivan was to meet challenges from his own brothers and, towards the end of his reign, he was to be embroiled in rivalries among his own direct descendants. It was not until late in the following century that Ivan IV, the Terrible, by his testament bequeathing virtually the whole realm to his heir and binding his younger son to obey his brother unto death, that any challenge to the throne, even by a blood-brother, came to be generally recognized as treason.

Ivan's brothers, while acknowledging his ascendancy, regarded him merely as the first or most senior among equals. Had Ivan been content to accept such a position, he might never have been faced with rebellions by his brothers. But his conception of the position and power of the Grand Prince allowed no place for equals; the apanage princes were his subjects and he early showed himself to be determined to limit their wealth and power. This was to be fully reflected in his new titles. His brothers were required to refer to him as *Gospodin*, meaning then "master" and as "Grand Prince of all Russia". His brothers also apparently assumed that, as apanage princes, they would share in the expansion of Muscovy and inherit equally or, at least proportionately, the estates of deceased members of the family. But this, too, was unacceptable to Ivan.

The first conflict came in 1472. Until that year the four brothers evidently co-operated in sending their troops to take part in the campaigns against Kazan and Novgorod, and in other ways. On 12 September 1472, however, Prince Yury, the eldest brother, died without heir, and Ivan at once absorbed his principality. Dmitri Donskoi had made provision in his will of 1389 that where one of his sons died the others would share his estate. Vasily II's will had been silent on this point, but the principle of dividing the estate among the surviving males of the family was held by many to be an established tradition, and Ivan's brothers clearly felt cheated by his action.

The strained relations after the death of Yury and Ivan's seizure of his entire estate made it timely and necessary to draw up agreements defining their relationships. Such deeds were, in fact, relics of the past when princes and boyars had freely entered into the service of the Grand Prince of their choice on terms agreed between them. The agreements made by Ivan with his two elder brothers—Prince Boris of Volok and Prince Andrei of Uglich—followed the old pattern. He made no agreement with his third brother, Prince Andrei of Vologda, who was apparently well-disposed and bequeathed his whole estate to him before dying in 1481. Princes Boris and Andrei gained no special concessions in their agreements with Ivan, apart from small additional lands, but they were apparently content. They sent their troops to serve in the campaign against Novgorod in 1477–78. Ivan appeared to enjoy friendly relations with Boris and visited him in his capital, Volokolamsk. But in 1480 at a time when Ivan was heavily engaged in Novgorod Princes Boris and Andrei rebelled against him.

Ivan had to be on his guard against enemies both within and without his realm. But the dangers of his childhood and the experience gained as the right hand of his blinded father had evidently trained him and developed his abilities. By nature he was immensely ambitious, hungry for wealth and power, but also cautious and practical. He was more able and farseeing than his predecessors and possessed the broad vision of a statesman, combined with extraordinary patience and tenacity. He has left the impression of a man who throughout most of his reign was master of himself, of his principality, and of the great developments which he directed. But, while these qualities may be discerned in his policies and the surviving records of the time, the man himself hardly emerges from the mists of history.

Although apparently less barbaric and cruel than many of his contemporaries, Ivan was not an attractive ruler. He was cold, ruthless, and calculating, and while he certainly held the loyalty and respect of his subjects, he did not command their love. He was too reserved and suspicious towards everyone, possibly as a result of the terrors of his childhood, and he was so forbidding in appearance that women sometimes fainted on coming face to face with him.

The only description of Ivan that has survived comes from the Italian traveller, Ambrogio Contarini, who passed through Moscow on his way to Persia. He noted that the Grand Prince "may be thirty-five years of age [he was nearly thirty-seven], he is tall, thin and handsome ..." Apparently he was rather stooped, for in some chronicles he was called *Gorbaty*, the Hunchback. Contarini also remarked that "it is his custom to visit the various parts of his dominions every year". This remark was misleading, however, for he did not delight in travel but preferred to remain in his palace, quietly planning and directing his policies. Indeed, his son-in-law, Stephen of Moldavia, held that he "increased his dominions while sitting at home and sleeping." The remark was charged with malice, but it was true that he seldom led his armies in person and was not one to seek glory in battle. He calculated every risk carefully and only when diplomacy and other methods had failed did he wage war to gain his objectives. Certain early chronicles have even suggested that he showed cowardice against the Tatars and, while such allegations are almost certainly false, there is no doubt that he would have considered any conduct, even flight in the face of the enemy, justified, if it served his purposes. Not dashing brilliance, but foresight, shrewdness, and tenacity enabled him to achieve so much in the midst of dangers and difficulties that would have daunted most men.

Ivan looked beyond these dangers, however, to the formation of the Russian nation, strongly centralized on the throne of Moscow and ruled by an absolute Tsar. It was an ambitious, even grandiose conception which he was perhaps the first to formulate, although the Russian movement towards unity under the strong rule of Moscow had begun long before his reign. He had, in fact, inherited the policy of extending Moscow's authority and recovering the Russian lands forming part of Lithuania. Ivan's greatness and achievement lay in his appreciation of the need for Russian unity and in the vision and ability he displayed in the pursuit of this great objective.

The nation which he envisaged was not limited to Great Russia, occupying the upper Volga region of which Moscow was the centre, but embraced all the lands occupied by Orthodox Russians. He claimed these lands on the ground that "since olden time from our ancient forebears, they have been our patrimony". His policy meant subduing or reaching some agreement with the Tatars and it made war with Lithuania inevitable, but Ivan was undeterred. His long rule of forty-four years was devoted to patient planning, tortuous diplomacy, and major wars waged on several fronts. Indeed, his singlemindedness lent to his reign a certain grandeur, and made him the most outstanding among the Grand Princes who expanded the minor principality of Moscow until it embraced the whole Russian nation.

Chapter Three

The Tatars 1462–87

FROM the outset of his reign Ivan III realized that he could not embark on war to recover the Russian lands in the west while Muscovy was exposed to Tatar attacks and while Novgorod and Pskov and four principalities remained beyond his control. Moreover, these problems were all inextricably involved with each other. The independent Russian princes and even minor Muscovite princes who resented the supremacy of the Grand Prince of Moscow turned to Lithuania or to the Golden Horde for help. Novgorod and Tver sought the aid of Lithuania, while Lithuania made alliances with the Golden Horde against Muscovy. For his part Ivan, the skilful opportunist, formed counter-alliances, disrupted the coalitions of his enemies, and in the last resort took military action.

The absorption of the independent principalities was to prove a minor problem. In 1463 the Princes of Yaroslavl ceded their rights to Ivan and swore allegiance to him. In the following year Ivan married his sister, Anna, to the young prince of Ryazan, which opened the way for him to absorb the principality at his convenience, and so slight was the danger of Ryazan opposing him that Ivan formally annexed only half of the principality, the other half remaining, nominally at least, independent. The princes of Rostov gave him no trouble and it was not until 1474 that he exacted an oath of allegiance from them. Tver was potentially more dangerous. The Grand Prince of Tver had served Ivan well, but later after negotiating a treaty with Moscow he had sought to save his independence by forming an alliance with Grand Prince Casimir of Lithuania. In August 1485 Ivan marched on Tver, captured the town and annexed the principality. Against Novgorod and Pskov, however, he moved with great caution, waiting nearly ten years before taking any action.

His first concern was nevertheless to deal with the Tatars of the Golden Horde, Kazan, and the Crimea. The Russians no longer feared the Tatars as in the 13th century when they had scourged the Russian lands. The Golden Horde, which had wielded suzerainty over Russia for more than 200 years, had been weakened by internal dissensions and by the devastation inflicted on them in 1395 by Tamerlane. About 1445 the Horde had been irreparably damaged by the breakaway of the Khanates of Kazan and the Crimea. The two new Khanates were also torn by rivalries and struggles for power. But in alliance the three Khanates were still strong enough to destroy Muscovy, and separately they could by their savage and persistent raiding wear down Russian defences and disrupt trade. Moreover the possibility of the Khans forming alliances with Moscow's western enemies was always a real threat.

The Khanate of Kazan, centred on the middle Volga, was the most immediate danger, because within easy striking distance of Moscow and able to halt the valuable trade with the east. In 1445 Mahmudek, who later in the same year became Khan of Kazan, had defeated the Muscovites near Suzdal, taking Vasily II prisoner. He had released the Grand Prince on payment of a huge ransom, but this resounding victory had raised the confidence of his Tatars and had encouraged him to regard Muscovy as still a vassal which should be compelled to pay regular tribute as in the past.

Seeking to weaken the position of the Grand Prince by stimulating rivalries, Mahmudek had plotted with Dmitri Shemyaka. But Vasily II had been able to counter these tactics when in 1446 Mahmudek's two brothers, Kasim and Yakub, fled with their armies to Moscow. They served Vasily II well, taking part in campaigns against Tatars of the Golden Horde and also against Dmitri Shemyaka. Kasim rendered outstanding service and was rewarded with grants of lands and the town of Gorodets, later known as Kasimov, on the Oka River. This Russian vassal Khanate was to prove of tremendous importance to the rulers of Moscow in years to come. Not only did it provide valuable defences on the Oka frontier against Tatar invasions from east and south, but also it was a reliable source of loyal Tatars who served as advisers, military leaders, and pro-Muscovite Khans.

In 1462, soon after ascending the throne, Ivan sent a force to reconnoitre in the Khanate of Kazan. For the next five years he took no further action, but in 1467 Mahmudek died and his son, Ibrahim, Kasim's nephew, became Khan. But his succession gave rise to disputes among the Tatars, some of whom approached Kasim, advising him to seize the throne to which he had better title than Ibrahim, especially as he had since married Mahmudek's widow. Seeking to take advantage of this dissension among the Tatars, Ivan in September 1467 sent a strong army, led by his three most able commanders, to capture Kazan and to make Kasim its Khan. But the expedition failed. The Muscovite troops, exhausted after a difficult march and by shortages of supplies, reached the Volga to find

Ibrahim with all his forces drawn up in strong positions, and the Muscovites beat a hurried retreat.

This failure spurred Ivan to despatch new expeditions. In December 1467, just two months after the retreat, he sent one force to lay waste the northern region and another from Murom and Nizhny Novgorod to plunder other parts of the Khanate. In the spring of the following year he massed an army at Vladimir for a major invasion, but for some reason this expedition was postponed, although detachments carried out several minor actions to harry the Tatars.

Early in 1469 Ivan was ready for a third time to mount a full-scale invasion of the Khanate, attacking from the north and west. Despite careful preparations this campaign also failed. But numerous minor actions took place during the following months. One force, led by a certain Ivan Runo, came close to capturing Kazan itself. Runo released all Christian prisoners in Tatar hands and set fire to the outskirts of the stronghold, and then retired. The subsequent fighting between Muscovites and Tatars was confused, especially as the people of Vyatka, who had sworn loyalty to Moscow in 1459, had later made a pact with the Khan agreeing to remain neutral. They proved unwilling to march with the Muscovite northern army against Kazan and this gravely hampered Muscovite operations.

Notwithstanding the failure of this summer campaign in 1469 Ivan later in the same year sent an even greater force against Kazan. The Muscovites invested the city and cut off its water supply. After only five days of siege the Khan sued for peace. Apparently he accepted all the conditions demanded by Prince Yury, Ivan's eldest brother, who was the chief Muscovite commander. Thus, while he had not succeeded in making his Tatar vassal, Kasim, Khan of Kazan, Ivan had by the pressure of his campaigns worn down Tatar resistance. He had won a valuable truce which freed him from attacks by the Kazan Tatars during the next nine years.

The Golden Horde was no more than a shadow of the vast Khanate established by Baty, but it still represented a threat to Muscovy and particularly to Ivan's policies. Ahmad, the Khan of the Golden Horde, prided himself on being directly descended from Chingiz Khan through his eldest son, Juchi, and he was determined to revive the suzerainty of the Khan over Muscovy as well as the annual payment of tribute.

According to legend, Ahmad, soon after becoming Khan, sent his envoys to Moscow with the demand that the Grand Prince should pay the customary tribute. But Ivan spat on the Khan's badge of authority when it was offered to him. This incident is said to have happened in 1480, but Ahmad had come to the throne at least twenty years earlier. He probably sent envoys to Moscow and, although Vasily II was then alive, Ivan III as co-ruler may have received them and rejected the Khan's demands. Ahmad then attacked Pereyaslavl in the Ryazan principality, but was repelled by Russian troops.

In 1465 Ahmad gathered his armies on the Don River in readiness for a major invasion of Muscovy. But there he was attacked and routed by Tatars from the Crimea, led by Khan Haji Girei, founder of the great Girei dynasty. From this conflict dated the bitter enmity between the two Khanates, which was to form the basis of Ivan's foreign policy and which ended only with the destruction of the Golden Horde.

In 1472 Ahmad again planned a massive invasion of Muscovy. The Grand Prince of Lithuania, Casimir, had sent envoys to him two years earlier, urging him to attack the Russians and promising his full support in a simultaneous campaign from the west. This time Ahmad did not march directly on Moscow through Kolomna, but moved westwards to the town of Aleksin, near the Lithuanian frontier. Evidently he was expecting that Casimir would join him with the Lithuanian army and that they would then advance together. But Casimir was too occupied elsewhere and sent no army. The Tatars burnt Aleksin to the ground and crossed the Oka, but then, faced by the Muscovite army 180,000 strong, which Ivan had sent, Ahmad hurriedly withdrew across the steppes.

Ivan did not underestimate the threat of the Golden Horde and shortly after Ahmad's invasion of 1472 he sent an envoy to Mengli-Girei, the second son of Haji-Girei, who had succeeded his father as Khan of the Crimea in 1469. His proposal was an alliance against the Golden Horde and Lithuania. But before this proposition could be discussed further Mengli-Girei had been dethroned by the Turkish Sultan.

The Ottoman Turks had in the 15th century become a mighty power, held in awe by Latin Christendom. In 1453 they had conquered Byzantium and they now ruled over Asia Minor and the Balkans and threatened to dominate the Mediterranean and Eastern Europe. Mohammed II, the Conqueror [1451–81], was one of the most outstanding of the Sultans and his reign was a period of aggressive expansion. In 1475 he embarked on a campaign to conquer the Crimea and secure the Black Sea as a Turkish lake, a "virgin" to be kept undefiled by Christian ships. The Ottoman fleet seized Kaffa, the chief city of the Crimea, and Mengli-Girei was cast into prison. The Sultan retained southern Crimea as a Turkish province, ruled from Kaffa by a governor. But he released the Khan and permitted him to rule as a Turkish vassal in northern Crimea. In 1476, however, Mengli-Girei was deposed by Ahmad who placed the Khanate in the hands of a relation. Apparently the Sultan was not greatly concerned by these struggles among the Tatars, his sole interest being that they should be obedient vassals. In 1478, however, he restored Mengli-Girei as Khan of northern Crimea.

Realizing that he could not count on his overlord, the Sultan, for support against his enemies, Mengli-Girei sought allies, especially against his most hated enemy, Ahmad. Alliance with Casimir of Lithuania held no attraction, for Casimir was on friendly terms with Ahmad, and Mengli-Girei's two brothers, who were among his most dangerous enemies, were under Casimir's protection. Mengli-Girei therefore made haste to send envoys to Moscow, announcing his restoration to the Khanate, referring to Ivan's approach to him six years earlier, and proposing an alliance. In April 1480 Ivan and Mengli-Girei agreed an offensive alliance against Lithuania, and a defensive alliance against the Golden Horde. The treaty suited Ivan who had no intention of invading Ahmad's vast territory and every intention of waging war against Casimir as soon as the time was ripe.

The agreement with the Khan was timely. For many months Ivan had been expecting Ahmad jointly with Casimir to attack Muscovy. Moreover, in January 1480 the Livonian Knights, probably in agreement with Casimir and Ahmad, invaded the Pskov region. Ivan's difficulties were aggravated further at this time by sedition in Novgorod and by a major internal crisis, caused by the revolt of two of his brothers. He put down the Novgorod rebellion, dealt with the revolt of his brothers [see pp. 55–7] and prepared anxiously to meet the dangerous threat of the joint Tatar-Lithuanian expedition.

In October 1480 Ahmad led his army to the banks of the Ugra River, a tributary of the Oka, west of

Kaluga. This time he moved farther west than in 1472, his purpose being to avoid the Russian defence lines on the northern bank of the Oka, and also to join forces with Casimir. The surviving accounts of Ahmad's campaign are confusing. It seems, however, that Russian opposition to his attempts to cross the Ugra was so strong that Ahmad finally retired and then made his camp on Lithuanian territory. Here he waited for the Lithuanian army to join him, but Casimir had been unable to win Polish support on which he counted and he was at this time distracted by massive Tatar raids, led by Mengli-Girei, into Podolia. Moreover among his Russian subjects Casimir found strong opposition to the campaigns against Muscovy.

When it was clear that he could count on no Lithuanian support, Ahmad laid waste the towns of the upper Oka region, taking considerable plunder. In November he led his army eastwards to Saray. He was now eager to reach the Khanate, for reports had come to him that Ivan had sent a detachment of Russian and Tatar horsemen to lay waste his territories. On the march he sent a letter to Ivan, demanding tribute and acknowledgment of the Khan's suzerainty, and also that the Russian vassal Khanate of Kasimov should be abolished.

Ivan's rejection of these demands and Ahmad's retreat from the Ugra River have usually been taken to mark the end of the Tatar yoke, which Russia had borne for nearly 250 years. But the Golden Horde had been crumbling and the Grand Princes had, in fact, ceased paying annual tribute and had refused recognition of the Khan's suzerainty since 1452, during the reign of Vasily II. Ahmad's attempts to revive the old relationship were in vain, and he himself was not destined to march again on Muscovy.

News of the rich plunder gathered by Ahmad in

Lithuania had spread. Ivak, Khan of the Tatar Khanate based on the town of Tyumen in Western Siberia, gathered his horsemen and secretly advanced towards Saray. On the march he was joined by a large force of Nogay Tatars from the steppelands east of the Volga. Ivak took the Golden Horde by surprise early on the morning of 6 January 1481. He himself made his way to the white tent of the Khan, where he found Ahmad still asleep, and killed him with his own hand. The Siberian and Nogay Tatars then sacked Saray and plundered the rest of the Khanate. Later Ivak sent envoys to Moscow with reports of this campaign, and Ivan in his delight sent the Khan rich presents.

The Golden Horde now stumbled towards disintegration. Ahmad's sons divided power among themselves, and the Khanate survived for only another twenty years. For Ivan the campaign of Ivak and the death of Ahmad were strokes of great good fortune, ridding him of a dangerous and aggressive enemy. But the defeat of the Horde did not mean that the Tatar danger was at an end or that he was free to embark on his great project of recovering the Russian lands from Lithuania. He applied himself to diplomacy and bribery to maintain his good relations with the Crimean Khan and to keep the Khanate of Kazan and the remnants of the Golden Horde from attacking Muscovy. The levies which the Grand Princes had made on their subjects to pay the Khan's tribute were continued and provided Ivan with funds with which to make presents to the Khans and to influential Tatars.

With the decline of the Golden Horde, the Khanate of Kazan once more became the main threat to Muscovy. But again events played into the hands of Ivan. About 1482 Khan Ibrahim died and was succeeded not by Mohammed-Amin or by Abdul-Letif, the sons of his chief wife, Nur-Sultan, but by Ilgam, the son of one of his minor wives. Nur-Sultan, who was an energetic and able woman, was incensed that her sons should have been deprived of the succession. Some three years after Ibrahim's death she married Mengli-Girei, Khan of the Crimean Khanate, and soon became his chief wife. She strongly supported her husband's alliance with Ivan who for his part, realizing that in her he had a strong ally, cultivated close relations with her and her family. Her plan to dethrone Ilgam and make her elder son, Mohammed-Amin, Khan of Kazan suited Ivan, who by rich presents won the support of a number of influential warrior-princes in Kazan. The two opposing parties of Ilgam and Mohammed-Amin plotted and conspired in Kazan for some years without result. But in 1486 Mohammed-Amin fled to Moscow and entreated Ivan to march on the Khanate to help him to assert his claim to the throne. In May 1487 Ivan's army laid siege to Kazan, and after fifty-two days of siege Ilgam surrendered and was imprisoned in Vologda. Mohammed-Amin then became Khan, as Ivan's vassal, and once more Ivan had contrived to neutralize the Khanate.

The alliance with Mengli-Girei, Khan of the Crimea, had served Ivan well against the Golden Horde and against Kazan. But he needed the Khan's support primarily against Lithuania, while the Khan had maintained the alliance mainly to aid him against the Golden Horde, for he was not directly threatened by Lithuania. Nevertheless he welcomed the freedom which alliance with Moscow gave him to raid the southern regions of Lithuania. In one large-scale raid on Kiev in 1482 the city and surrounding country were so terribly devastated that they did not recover for many years. These raids provided the Tatars with rich plunder, especially gold taken from the churches and princely homes. But the chief purpose of the raids was to capture men, women, and children. Taken to Kaffa they were sold in the slave-markets, and shipped to Egypt, Turkey, and to countries of the western Mediterranean.

While the Ukrainian lands remained part of Lithuania, the Tatar raids served Ivan's purposes in that they frequently distracted Casimir from attacking Muscovy. The time was soon to come, however, when a large part of the Ukraine had been recovered and become part of Muscovy, and the Tatar raids then caused misgivings in Moscow.

Chapter Four

Marriage with Sofia Palaeologa

IVAN married twice. His first wife was Princess Maria, sister of his neighbour, the Grand Prince of Tver. She bore him a son, Ivan Ivanovich, known as Ivan Molodoi [the Young], but in 1467 she died. Ivan granted this son the title of Grand Prince and recognized him as his co-ruler and heir, but this did not calm the general anxiety over the succession in an age when life was often cut short. Ivan, himself only twenty-seven years old at the time of his wife's death, nevertheless showed no haste in seeking another wife.

In February 1469, however, proposals came from an unexpected quarter. Pope Paul II through Cardinal Bessarion offered Ivan the hand of his ward, Zoe Palaeologa. This princess was the niece of the last Byzantine Emperor, Constantine XI, who had perished on the walls of Constantinople, fighting against the Turks in 1453. His brother, Thomas Palaeologus, had been Despot of Morea, but had fled from the approaching Turks in 1460 and had found refuge in Italy where he had died soon afterwards. The Pope had taken the three children under his care. To supervise their education he appointed Cardinal Bessarion, a Greek scholar and Roman Catholic convert, who had always laboured zealously to bring about the union of the Eastern and Western Churches. Zoe was about fourteen years old when she came to Rome and she lived there some ten years.

In proposing this marriage, the Pope had two purposes. First, he believed that Zoe, who had accepted the Union of Florence and was a convert to Roman Catholicism, well schooled in the faith by Bessarion, would further the cause of Rome in Muscovy. He fervently hoped that she would influence the Grand Prince in favour of the revival of the union of the churches. Second, he was anxiously seeking allies against the Ottoman Turks, whose steady advance into south-eastern Europe gave rise to recurrent crises in Latin Christendom. Many feared that the Turkish conquest of Europe was imminent. Popes, princes, and churchmen appealed for a united Europe to meet this threat, and the lingering mystique of the crusades attracted many to the idea of a new crusade against the Turkish enemies of civilization and of true religion. Reports of agents had encouraged the Pope to believe that Ivan would be a strong and active ally against the Turks. On both counts the Pope miscalculated grievously, but Ivan's marriage with Zoe Palaeologa was to have great significance in the history of Russia. [See Appendix 3.]

To Ivan the Pope's proposal was attractive. The prestige of the Byzantine Emperors had always stood high among the Russians, who had looked upon Constantinople as the capital of the world. Even after the Turkish conquest Byzantium had retained a compelling glamour for the Russians. Marriage with the niece of the last Emperor would undoubtedly enhance the dignity of the Grand Prince and of his principality.

Against this advantage Ivan had to recognize that the prospect of Zoe as Grand Princess would disturb many of his subjects. She was the ward of the Pope whom they feared and hated. She was a Greek and had supported the Union of Florence, which was anathema to all Orthodox Russians. At the Council of Florence in 1439 the Metropolitan of Moscow, a Greek named Isidore, had accepted on behalf of Russian Orthodoxy the reunion of the Eastern and Western Churches and the principle of papal supremacy. Both decisions had horrified the Russians. On his return Isidore was instantly deposed by a Russian Synod and forced to flee for his life. A declaration of the complete autonomy of the Russian Church had followed and a Russian, Iona, Bishop of Ryazan, had been elected Metropolitan. These events were alive in the minds of all Russians, and Ivan himself was too astute not to realize the danger that his proposed marriage might stir these memories to a popular fury. With his usual caution he consulted earnestly with the Metropolitan, with his mother, and with the Boyar Council. He then sent to Rome a certain Ivan Friazin, an Italian whose proper name was Gian Battista della Volpe, whom he had appointed to take charge of his Mint and to carry out other tasks. Volpe discussed the proposal with the Pope and with Cardinal Bessarion, and with Zoe who agreed to the marriage. He returned to Moscow with a portrait of Zoe and reported on the general approval for the marriage. Ivan consulted further with the Metropolitan and others. Then, putting aside such religious scruples as he may have had, he decided to marry her.

In January 1472 Volpe set out again for Rome, this time to bring Zoe to Moscow. He was received by Pope Sixtus IV, Pope Paul II having died in the previous year, and on 1 June 1472 in a solemn ceremony, with Volpe acting as proxy, Zoe and Ivan III were betrothed. Later in the month Zoe, accompanied by Volpe, by the papal legate, Cardinal Antonio Bonumbre, and by a numerous and impressive suite, set out for Moscow.

Zoe probably left Rome without special regrets. She

had received an advanced education and had grown up in the vital, exciting, cultured world of an Italy where the ferment of the Renaissance was about to burst into flower. At the same time she was an orphan and homeless, dependent on the charity of the Pope, and neither she nor her brothers were ever allowed to forget it. Cardinal Bessarion enjoined on them constantly to be grateful to their benefactors and industrious in their studies. He stressed that they should think of themselves as paupers, not as the children of an illustrious family. But Zoe certainly did not forget her imperial origins, and she was always to think of herself before all else as a Byzantine princess. Even in 1498, after twenty-six years as the wife of Ivan III, she inscribed herself on an altar-cloth which she embroidered not as Grand Princess of Muscovy, but as Princess of Tsargrad, the Russian name for Constantinople.

The Turkish conquest of Byzantium and the Balkans had so disrupted communications that Zoe and her party could not proceed by the shortest route to Moscow, but travelled by way of Germany and the Baltic. She landed at Reval and thence travelled by land to Pskov and Novgorod. In both cities the Russians welcomed her warmly, and they were favourably impressed when they saw her worship in their churches and reverence their ikons. What disturbed them was the behaviour of Cardinal Antonio, who, clad in scarlet, was preceded by an attendant bearing a crucifix, the "latin cross", hated as deepest heresy by Orthodox Russians. The approach of the party to Moscow threatened a crisis. Metropolitan Philip declared that he would leave the city, if the Cardinal profaned it with this crucifix, and many boyars objected vigorously. Finally, Ivan sent a boyar to the Cardinal, forbidding him to uncover the crucifix in the city.

On 12 November 1472 Zoe Palaeologa entered Moscow. On that day she was received into the Orthodox Church under the name of Sofia, and she and Ivan were married by the Orthodox rites. The Cardinal remained in the background and for him it was a distressing and bewildering time. He had seen Sofia readily abandon Roman Catholicism and had witnessed the fervour of the Orthodox Russians. He did not attempt, therefore, to broach the revival of the Union of Florence, but he stayed in Moscow for some weeks, trying without success to persuade Ivan to march against the Ottoman Porte.

Sofia was apparently untroubled by these setbacks to the papal mission, and concentrated on adopting her new country. She proved remarkably adaptable. She had come from the most civilized city in Europe at that time to one of the most primitive, but she settled down quickly and apparently without complaint. She had evidently seized on the opportunity to escape from the oppressive dependence on benefactors, and she welcomed the dignity, power, and even independence of her new position. She held her own court where she was encouraged to receive foreign visitors. Contarini stated that he called on her at the request of Ivan himself, and he recorded that "she treated me with great kindness and courtesy, and entreated me earnestly to recommend her to my Illustrious Seignory".

Sofia was described by one visitor who saw her in 1472 as beautiful, but another visitor, present at the time, considered her to be distressingly fat. Whether ugly or beautiful, she was undoubtedly a most intelligent woman, skilled in dissembling her feelings and in intrigue. Among the Russians, even in succeeding generations, she was credited with great and even sinister powers over Ivan III. Highly educated by the standards of the time in Europe, and fluent in several languages, her abilities must have seemed exceptional to the illiterate boyars of Muscovy, whose wives were ignorant creatures, living closely guarded in seclusion.

Many Russians, while dutifully welcoming her on her arrival in Moscow, nevertheless eyed Sofia with deep suspicion. Ivan Molodoi, Ivan III's son by his first wife, had good reason to resent his new stepmother, for her children might displace him from the succession. Indeed, it seems that Ivan Molodoi, aged sixteen at the time of Sofia's arrival, may have given vent to his feelings. Contarini recorded that in 1476 he was "not in great favour on account of his bad conduct", but unfortunately he gave no explanation and merely added, "I might mention other things, but it would take too long."

In the first four years of her marriage, Sofia bore Ivan two daughters and Contarini thought, mistakenly, that she was again pregnant when he saw her in 1476. It was not, however, until three years later that her first son, Vasily, was born. Meantime Ivan Molodoi had married the Moldavian princess, Elena Stepanova, who in 1483 gave birth to a son, named Dmitri. In 1490 Ivan Molodoi died, and Sofia's son, Vasily, and Elena's son, Dmitri, were as the son and grandson of Ivan III equally claimants to the succession, for the Muscovite law of succession was far from clear. Towards the end of his reign this rivalry was to cause confusion and conflict.

During the 1470s the dignity and surroundings of the Grand Prince began to undergo a transformation. Moscow had developed into a great sprawling city, but built almost entirely of timber, and whole suburbs were frequently destroyed by fire. A serious fire in 1468 was followed by another in the next year which burnt to the ground nearly all the buildings within the Kremlin. Skilled in the use of timber, the Muscovite artisans quickly replaced the destroyed buildings, but still using timber. The Cathedral of the Dormition [Uspensky Sobor], built of timber over a century earlier, was collapsing. In 1472 the Metropolitan commissioned two Russian masters to erect a new cathedral, but their building collapsed in the course of erection. The Grand Prince then summoned masters from Pskov, but they were not entrusted with the task. At this time, probably on Sofia's persuasion, Ivan decided to engage skilled masters from Italy for this important undertaking. Ivan's agents found many masters of building in Venice, but only one who was prepared to come to Muscovy. This was Aristotle Fioraventi who brought with him his son, Andrei, and an apprentice, named Peter. He began work on the cathedral in 1475 and completed it four years later. Fioraventi, like so many of the Renaissance masters, was skilled in many fields, and while in Muscovy he cast cannon and bells, minted money, and built bridges for the Grand Prince.

Ivan now sent his agents to Italy, Venice, and to the Emperor to engage more experts. In 1487 he commissioned a Venetian, named Mark, to build him a palace, and in 1491 Mark completed the Granovitaya, or Faceted Palace, which was used for formal occasions, such as the audiences of foreign ambassadors. Ivan also had a residence of stone erected for himself, but this was no sooner completed than it was damaged by fire. In 1482–91 masters from Pskov erected a new cathedral of the Annunciation. In fact, during these years ceaseless building went on in Moscow and especially in the Kremlin, where several boyars built themselves mansions of brick, and where new stone walls were erected. Moscow was indeed being transformed and becoming a capital worthy of the powerful Grand Prince.

At the same time Ivan was adopting grandiose titles

and court ceremonial which reflected his conception of the new significance and role of the Grand Prince of Moscow. They were not merely exercises in pomp and ceremony, but an expression of the outlook of the ruler of an emerging power. On his accession his title of Grand Prince had signified that he was the senior and ruling prince of Moscow. Other Muscovite princes acknowledged this senior position, but they did so grudgingly. Many of the princes at his court could trace their families back to the same or to equally illustrious forebears, and they saw themselves as not inferior to him and not without title to the throne. But he contemptuously dismissed such pretensions, for as Grand Prince he saw himself as far above them in dignity and power.

In his relations with Western courts Ivan had used the title of "Sovereign of All Russia", but after finally discarding the Mongol–Tatar yoke in 1480 he began referring to himself as "Tsar of all Russia", sometimes adding "Samoderzhets", the Russian equivalent of the Byzantine title of "Autocrat". "Tsar", a Slav contraction of the Latin "Caesar", had at this time none of its later meaning of a sovereign wielding unlimited power; it signified merely a ruler who owed no allegiance or obedience to any other foreign authority and who paid tribute to none.

In his new use of Tsar and Autocrat, Ivan was at first proclaiming merely that he was an independent sovereign, ruling over the domains listed in his full title. Soon, however, these titles became more elevated. "Ivan, by the grace of God, Sovereign of All Russia" reflected the new religious basis to the Tsarish power. The Russian church had always given its fullest support to the Princes of Moscow in their policy of uniting the Russian lands under their sole rule. But Ivan's title drew its full meaning from the Byzantine belief in the God-given authority of the autocrat.

When towards the end of Ivan's reign, the German Emperor Frederick III sent his envoys to Moscow to propose the marriage of one of Ivan's daughters with his nephew and to offer him the title of King, Ivan replied proudly : "We by the grace of God have been sovereigns over our domains from the beginning, from our first forebears, and our right we hold from God, as did our forebears. We pray to God that it may be granted to us and our children for all time to continue as sovereigns as we are at present, and as in the past we have never needed appointment from anyone, so now we do not desire it."

Thus Ivan regarded himself as autocrat of Muscovy and national ruler of the whole Russian land, and also as the successor of the Eastern Emperors. He fully realized that Sofia could not have brought with her the legal title to the throne of Byzantium. Her elder brother, Andrew, had, in fact, sold his rights to the throne three times over, each time to a different person. He visited Moscow twice and may well have offered to sell his rights there, but no record exists of his having done so. In any case Ivan had no need to claim his dubious legal title when he was assuming the heritage of Byzantium. His marriage with Sofia had enabled him to surround his throne with the aura of Byzantium, and he was astute in introducing imperial trappings to give permanence to this aura. He promoted the idea of the Grand Prince of Moscow holding power from God and as the heir of the Byzantine Emperors. It was significant that in the late 1490s the double-headed eagle, the imperial Byzantine emblem, came to be used on his seals, and was soon to become established as the crest of Tsarist Russia.

In the coronation of Ivan's grandson, Dmitri, in

1498 the new conception of the power and dignity of the Grand Prince of Moscow was elaborately expressed. The ceremony closely followed Byzantine ritual for the installation of the secondary ruler, and the full Byzantine regalia was used. The Metropolitan conducted the ceremony, but it was Ivan himself who placed the regalia upon his grandson, bestowing on him the succession and blessing him in his office. In this Ivan showed that he believed himself to be able to convey the office and power granted to him by God, and it was but a short step from this to the idea of the divine nature of the sovereign, a conception which was already gathering strength among the Russians.

The Grand Prince was, moreover, becoming more remote from his subjects and elevated above them. Formerly, relations between Grand Prince and subjects had been marked by a simple directness. Peasants, townsmen, and churchmen addressed their Grand Prince with a man-to-man frankness on occasion. In 1480 Ivan himself had suddenly left his troops on the Oka River, where they were drawn up in readiness to repel a Tatar invasion, and had returned to Moscow. There he had met with strong and open criticism that he was failing in his duty to defend his people. Vassian, the Archbishop of Rostov, bluntly called him a coward and deserter. But this simple frank attitude even on the part of a senior churchman, towards the Grand Prince, was soon to become unthinkable, and the growing elevation of the sovereign above his subjects gave strength to the idea of his divine nature, an idea which Ivan IV, the Terrible, established.

Legends were created in support of these new pretensions. In the 15th century the Grand Princes began to trace their family descent back to the Roman Emperors. One legend, apparently composed later in Ivan's reign, related that the Emperor Augustus had divided his empire among his family, granting to his brother, Prus, a kingdom on the banks of the Nieman River, which came to be known as Prussia. The Varangian founder of Russia, Rurik, was, it was claimed, directly descended from Prus and thus he and his successors, the Muscovite rulers, were descended from the Roman Emperors.

Another legend, composed at this time, concerned the Kievan prince, Vladimir Monomakh. It related that Vladimir, having been crowned in Kiev, despatched troops to attack the Emperor, Constantine Monomachus, in Constantinople. But Constantine sent the Greek Metropolitan to Kiev with gifts and his own crown to propose peace so that all Orthodoxy might dwell in harmony "under the combined power of our Tsardom and of your great autocracy 'Great Rus'". Vladimir was then crowned with Constantine's crown and took the name of Monomakh, divinely ordained Tsar of Great Russia. The *Shapka Monomakha* [the Cap of Monomachus] was thereafter always used as the coronation crown of the Tsars of Russia.

This legend furthered the claim of the Muscovite Grand Prince to be heir to the Byzantine Emperors in the fullest sense of being absolute in both temporal and ecclesiastical spheres. Supporting this claim there arose after the fall of Constantinople in 1453 the legend of Moscow as the Third Rome. The theory found its clearest expression in the pronouncement of Pilotheus, a monk of a Pskov monastery, who in a letter to Ivan III's son, Vasily III, wrote:

"I wish to add a few words on the present Orthodox Empire of our ruler; he is on earth the sole Emperor [Tsar] of the Christians, the leader of the Apostolic Church which stands no longer in Rome or in Constantinople, but in the blessed city of

Moscow. She alone shines in the whole world brighter than the sun ... All Christian Empires are fallen and in their stead stands alone the Empire of our ruler in accordance with the prophetical books. Two Romes have fallen, but the third stands, and a fourth there will not be."

This claim made a tremendous emotional appeal to the devout people of the emerging Russian nation. It did not inhibit Ivan in his policy of seeking peace and even alliance with the Muslim Turks, and it did not draw him into the error of seeking to assert authority over the Eastern Empire which was now in Turkish hands. But the theory of the Third Rome added greatly to the prestige and power of Moscow as the centre of the nation, as the holy city which was the capital of the Russian autocrat.

Chapter Five

Novgorod the Great

IN the midst of his complicated relations with the Tatars and his longer-term plans against Lithuania, Ivan could not ignore the three city-states of Pskov, Vyatka, and Novgorod. Their continued independence stood as an obstacle to his first great objective—the unification of the whole of Great Russia under Moscow's rule. Pskov and Vyatka were both important cities, but Novgorod dwarfed them in its extent, wealth, and significance. Moreover, her dominions, lying between Muscovy and the Baltic Sea, were of direct importance to Ivan's policies.

Lord Novgorod the Great, as the republic was respectfully known, was the centre of commerce between east and west, and in many ways overshadowed Moscow at this time. The city itself was situated just five kilometres beyond the northern tip of Lake Ilmen, and the republic lay in the basin of the Volkhov River. It was a region of marshes, lakes, and dense forests, divided by large rivers, which flowed into Lake Ilmen. All of these rivers, of which the Volkhov, Msta, Lovat, and Shelon were the most important, were navigable by small boats and barges, and provided ready communications with the capital.

The empire of Novgorod was divided into five vast provinces which centred on the heartland. The Vodskaya and Obonezhskaya provinces stretched to the north, the former to the Gulf of Finland and embracing

44

the Finnish lands beyond Lake Ladoga, the latter extended north-east to the White Sea. The Shelonskaya province lay to the west, reaching to the city-republic of Pskov. The Derevskaya and Bezhetskaya provinces were to the south-east and east of Novgorod. Each province was ruled by a governor, chosen from one of the most senior families of Novgorod, and exercising very wide powers.

The city, standing on both banks of the Volkhov River, was divided into the merchant quarter on the east bank and the Sofiiskaya quarter on the west bank, and joined by a bridge. In the merchant quarter was organized the administrative and trading business of the city, while the Sofiiskaya side, named after its renowned cathedral, was the religious and cultural centre. Novgorod's significance was apparent from the fact that it had its own Archbishop who was second only to the Metropolitan of Moscow in prestige and authority. Moreover, in the 15th and 16th centuries Novgorod was culturally the richest city in Russia. Fine arts and crafts were practised there. Books were translated and copied by its monks, and new works, dealing principally with the lives of the saints, were produced.

In the 11th century Novgorod had acknowledged the authority of Kiev, but as the power of Kiev had declined in the following century Novgorod had asserted its independence. The Mongol invasion of the 13th century which had destroyed Kiev and other towns in Russia had not harmed Novgorod. The city had been required to pay its share of the tribute levied by the Khan, but it had, in fact, benefited during the Mongol domination, because the Khans had guaranteed the city's political and trading privileges. Indeed, Novgorod's trade in the Baltic especially with the Hanseatic League, with the northern lands, forming part of her empire, and along the Volga to the Caspian Sea had flourished during this period.

Second only to trade, the people of Novgorod treasured the freedom and autonomy which they had achieved during these centuries. They had developed a constitution which was republican and to a certain degree democratic. They had the right to choose a prince from any one of the princely families in Russia. Usually they chose the Grand Prince of Moscow, but the powers of their princes were severely restricted. On election he had to swear a special oath and sign a contract, undertaking to protect Novgorod's institutions and to exercise only those powers granted to him. He could not own estates within the central republic; he could not seek to influence the election of the officials, nor could he dismiss them without the approval of the assembly of the citizens, which was known as the *veche*. In fact, he was little more than a puppet with certain judicial and military functions. Even his residence lay outside the city and he was regarded by all as an outsider, not as a citizen.

Power in the republic was vested in the *veche*. All the men of Novgorod had the right to take part in its gatherings and to cast their votes. Decisions had to be unanimous which meant in practice that minorities had to bow to the will of the majority. When the *veche* was fairly evenly divided on any matter, the parties often resorted to fisticuffs and the meetings would break up in disorder. The citizens were grouped in this assembly according to the communities of boyars, merchants, artisans of the various trades, and the poorer people, into which the city was divided and subdivided. Conflicts often arose between these different groups. The basic division was, however, between those who ate white bread and those who ate rye bread, between the rich and the poor.

The wealthy noble class provided the members of the Boyar Council which met in the palace of the Archbishop who presided. It wielded considerable powers and its rights to prepare the matters to be submitted to the *veche* meant that it could control its meetings to a large extent. Nevertheless, it was the *veche* which annually elected the *posadnik* or mayor, as well as the commander of the city's troops and chief judge. Both of these officials had wide authority and were chosen from the upper class. The *veche* also nominated the Archbishop who played an important part in the secular affairs of the republic. The government of Novgorod and its empire thus lay in the hands of the *veche*, the Boyar Council, and the chief officials elected by the citizens. The prince, holding little more than nominal office, was subjected to their strict control.

This treasured independence of Novgorod was, however, insecure. For food, trade, and, most important of all, for defence the republic had to depend on its neighbours. The lands of both the republic itself and its possessions were infertile, and the climate so severe that they could not be cultivated and were valued only for such natural resources as tar, iron ore, flax, and for hunting and fishing. The people of Novgorod relied for staple foods on imports of wheat and other grains from the more fertile lands to the east. So great was their dependence on these imports that Novgorod was on occasion faced with famine when neighbours prevented grain deliveries along the Volga and other rivers. Similarly their trade was dependent upon the free flow of traffic eastwards and southwards, and particularly down the Volga to the Caspian Sea.

The chief reason for Novgorod's vulnerability, however, was the failure to build up and maintain a military force, capable of defending the republic against Russian principalities in the east and against Lithuanians, Swedes, and Germans in the west. The first duty of the prince was to defend the city and its empire, but the people were so suspicious that the Grand Prince of Moscow, usually the elected prince, was forbidden to keep a permanent force in the city and such help as might be sent from Moscow would come too late. Mercenary troops were engaged on occasions and Novgorod made some attempt to establish a regular army. The church provided a cavalry force and in time of crisis all citizens were mobilized. This appeared to give the city a massive army, but in practice it was an undisciplined and ill-equipped force, incapable of standing against much smaller enemy forces. In 1456, for example, 200 Muscovite troops are said to have put 5,000 Novgorodtsi to flight.

Clinging to their trade and independence, but looking to one or other of their neighbours for protection, Novgorodtsi viewed with misgiving the growing power of Muscovy. They tried to find security in alliances with Lithuania, but this policy gave rise to dissension among them. The boyar and upper class as a whole favoured alliance with Lithuania as the best means of preserving their independence and wealth. On the other hand the clergy had misgivings that a Lithuanian alliance would expose the church to Roman Catholic persecution. To the lower classes, good relations with Muscovy meant plentiful and cheap bread, and they had much less to lose by Muscovite domination. Alliance with Lithuania was therefore unpopular with them. Such were broadly the divisions among the Novgorodtsi, most of whom were anxious to avoid conflicts with either of their powerful enemies.

During the first part of the 15th century Lithuania made strenuous efforts to annex Novgorod, but this pressure ceased in 1430 on the death of Grand Prince Vitovt, Svidrigaylo, his successor, was plagued by internal troubles and relieved to sign an "eternal peace" with Novgorod. But at this stage Muscovite pressure revived. Vasily II considered that Novgorod should be brought under the authority of Moscow, and the fact that his cousin and rival, Dmitri Shemyaka, after being defeated by Muscovite troops in 1452, was given refuge in Novgorod, strengthened his determination to subjugate the city to his rule. In the following year Shemyaka, poisoned by Muscovite agents, was given a full state funeral in Novgorod and to Vasily this was a further affront.

In 1456 Vasily marched on Novgorod and his small Muscovite detachment put the Novgorod cavalry to flight. The Archbishop was sent to negotiate and the treaty, concluded with Vasily and his son, Ivan III, then aged sixteen, placed limits on the city's independence. The *veche* was no longer to issue charters without the approval of the prince and the city was not to offer asylum to political offenders, fleeing from Moscow. Furthermore the new conception of treason was introduced into Novgorod's relations with Moscow, for any assistance rendered to Moscow's enemies was to be considered in future as a political offence against the Grand Prince.

This treaty lay heavily upon the people of Novgorod, who were determined to free themselves from its restrictive clauses. Marfa Boretskaya, a remarkable woman who headed the boyar party which sought alliance with Casimir of Lithuania, plotted actively to throw off the restraints imposed by the Grand Prince of Moscow. This pro-Lithuanian party grew in strength and began openly defying the Grand Prince. Lithuania failed to respond to their appeals for help, probably because Casimir was reluctant to become involved in war with Muscovy. But two rebel Muscovite princes, living in Lithuania, agreed to go to the aid of Novgorod. They were Ivan Andreevich of Mozhaisk, who had been involved personally in the blinding of Vasily II, and Ivan Dmitrievich, son of Shemyaka. Moreover, the boyar party in 1470 invited Prince Mikhail Olelkovich, whose father and grandfather had been princes of Kiev and who was representative of many of the Russians living under Lithuanian rule, to come to Novgorod with his force and to help defend the city.

Relations between Novgorod and Moscow were aggravated further by religious conflict. In 1470 Archbishop Iona died and the *veche* chose as his successor a certain Feofil whom Moscow approved. But then in Novgorod violent opposition erupted against Feofil going to Moscow to be ordained by the Metropolitan. The boyar party insisted that he should be blessed by the Archbishop of Kiev, Grigori. Feofil refused to go to Kiev. Grigori had been ordained by the Greek Uniate Patriarch and by the Pope in Rome and only subsequently by the Orthodox Greek Patriarch. Moscow refused to recognize Grigori, regarding him as a creature of the Pope. The boyar party attempted to have Pimen, who was prepared to go to Kiev, ordained in the place of Feofil, but this attempt to change the decision of the *veche* caused a further outcry.

The boyar party nevertheless succeeded in the end, mainly by the use of liberal bribes, in persuading the *veche* to vote in favour of the alliance with Casimir. The treaty was negotiated and signed in February 1471. Under it Novgorod acknowledged the sovereignty of King Casimir of Lithuania–Poland, although he was in fact acting only in his capacity as Grand Prince of Lithuania. But Casimir had to give extensive undertakings to respect the rights of the republic and he undertook to defend it with the full force of the Lithuanian army against Moscow. The treaty was indeed so one-sided that it can hardly have aroused much enthusiasm in Casimir who apparently did not ratify it.

Ivan III at once took action. In the spring of 1471 he summoned an assembly of representatives of church and state, aristocracy and gentry, which may be taken as a forerunner of the Assembly of the Land [Zemsky Sobor] which was to become prominent in the reign of his grandson, Ivan the Terrible. At this assembly it was decided to march on Novgorod without delay. Philip, the Metropolitan of Moscow, sent formal warnings to Novgorod against forming an alliance with Casimir and accepting the authority of Grigori, Archbishop of Kiev. He enjoined them to obey the Grand Prince. His warnings had no effect. Ivan also sent an envoy, calling on his "subjects" of Novgorod to cease from rebellion against him and to show obedience. This approach was also without effect.

Ivan then sent a declaration of war and in June 1471 three armies set out from Moscow. The people of Novgorod, still divided among themselves, were now in serious difficulties. They could expect no help from Casimir who was at this time taken up with Czech and Hungarian affairs. Pskov refused help and sided with Moscow. The Livonian Knights turned deaf ears to their pleas for help.

The surviving chronicles give confused and conflicting accounts of the campaign. Apparently in June Muscovite and Tatar forces invaded Novgorod territory at three points. Ivan himself reached Torzhok towards the end of the month and was joined there by forces from Tver and Pskov. The decisive engagement took place on the banks of the Shelon River to the south-west of Novgorod. The Muscovite advance guard of 5,000 mounted troops routed the Novgorod army 40,000 strong. The Novgorodtsi lost 12,000 killed and 2,000 captured. In the Pechora and Dvina regions Muscovite forces won further victories. Thus both on the home front and in its dominions Novgorod suffered disastrous defeats.

The Archbishop-elect, Feofil, led the Novgorod delegation to Ivan's camp near the mouth of the Shelon River to sue for peace. Ivan had already executed Dmitri, son of Marfa Boretskaya, and other leaders of the pro-Lithuanian party who had been taken captive. But he sent most of his prisoners back to Novgorod where they strengthened the pro-Muscovite party which was now in the ascendant.

The peace which Ivan granted was, however, fairly lenient. At least the Novgorodtsi were allowed to continue calling themselves "free men" and they retained a semblance of independence. Ivan annexed only a small part of their northern empire and imposed a fine of 15,500 rubles which they could readily afford to pay. But now, in addition to cancelling their treaty with Casimir, they had to swear never to seek alliance with the ruler of Lithuania and Poland or to accept Lithuanian princes into their service. Other clauses in the earlier treaty with Moscow, made in 1456, were repeated. Their church had to accept the authority of the Metropolitan of Moscow who alone could consecrate their Archbishops. Further their charter of justice was reissued under the seal of the Grand Prince.

Although so moderate, this peace lay heavily upon the Novgorodtsi. They were for a time united in seeking to preserve as much as possible of their old rights and institutions. But soon conflicts revived among them. The boyar party, intending to rebel against Moscow's authority at the first opportunity, used bribery and even force to compel the support of other classes. Reports of the increasing uneasiness in Novgorod began to reach Moscow, and Ivan decided to spend the winter of 1475–76 in the city. He was received by the people with every display of loyalty. He heard complaints and accepted gifts from all classes. He had several leaders of the pro-Lithuanian faction arrested, including Feodor Boretsky, another of Marfa's sons. His visit won him the support of the middle and lower classes and, having restored order to the city, he returned to Moscow towards the end of January 1476.

For some months Novgorod seemed outwardly peaceful. But then conflicts erupted afresh. Delegations began arriving in Moscow to plead their causes. In March 1477 the pro-Muscovite party secured the vote of the *veche* in favour of accepting the full sovereignty of the Grand Prince over the city and its possessions. Also in this month two minor officials arrived in Moscow and in their petition they addressed Ivan not as *Gospodin* [meaning Lord, as then used], the traditional form of address, but as *Gosudar* [Sovereign]. It is not known with any certainty whether these two officials were sent by the Archbishop to speak in the name of Novgorod, whether they came merely to present personal petitions, or whether they were prompted secretly by Muscovite agents to address the Grand Prince in this form.

Ivan seized on their use of *Gosudar* as a voluntary confirmation that Novgorod accepted him as its sovereign. Without delay he sent envoys who announced to the assembled *veche* that he would accept the proferred sovereignty. His conditions were that he should have full judicial authority in the republic and its dominions, that local officials should not seek to set aside his commands, and that his residence should be within the city, not outside, in Gorodishche where the elected prince had always been required to reside.

Novgorod was now in an uproar. Many boyars and others again proposed alliance with Casimir, although they had formally sworn not to revive such an alliance. Ivan's envoys were held for six weeks before being allowed to return to Moscow and then they took with them the reply that the Novgorodtsi would not recognize Ivan as their sovereign, but only as their lord, and that they adhered to the treaty of 1471.

To Ivan this was a personal affront as well as a setback to his policy. On 30 September [1477] he sent a declaration of war and nine days later he marched. Towards the end of November his massive army, reinforced by Kasimov Tatar horsemen and troops from Tver, stood before Novgorod. The people had fortified their city and, refusing Muscovite demands to surrender, they seemed prepared for a long siege. Always cautious, Ivan did not attempt to take the city by storm, but planned to starve the people into submission. He did not have long to wait. In December Novgorod capitulated and soon afterwards her leaders and all her citizens took the oath of allegiance to him as their *Gosudar* or Sovereign.

Ivan now imposed conditions which meant the end of Novgorod's independence. He required the dissolution of the *veche* and the handing over of its bell, used to summon the citizens and treasured as the symbol of Novgorod's freedom. The office of *posadnik* or mayor was abolished. Then came the territorial demands against which the Novgorod delegates protested in vain. Ivan annexed all the northern and eastern dominions and the rural parts of Torzhok province, and the Archbishop surrendered ten rural districts from his see. The provinces remaining to Novgorod had to pay tribute to the Grand Prince. Ivan had thus, as he jubilantly claimed, "Subjected my patrimony Novgorod the Great to my entire will and had become sovereign there just as in Moscow."

Bereft of most of her dominions and completely subjugated, Novgorod still struggled feebly to recover something of her former freedom and prestige. Certain boyars, encouraged by Archbishop Feofil, began plotting to secure assistance from Lithuania. Casimir had failed them in 1471, but he was now seeking allies against Moscow and in 1479 had formed an alliance with Ahmad, Khan of the Golden Horde, to mount a joint attack on Muscovy. The Novgorod conspirators also made contact with Ivan's brothers, Prince Andrei of Uglich and Prince Boris of Volok, who were already secretly negotiating with Casimir.

In October 1479 Ivan learnt of this conspiracy. He at once set out with a small force and this time he gave no warning in a formal declaration of war. The boyars of Novgorod nevertheless learnt in advance of the approach of the Muscovite troops. They manned their defences and refused to surrender. But then, realizing that resistance was useless, they submitted and pleaded for mercy.

This conspiracy, combining against him his own brothers as well as Lithuania and the Golden Horde, was too dangerous to be treated leniently. Ivan entered Novgorod on 15 January 1480. Archbishop Feofil was deposed and imprisoned in the Chudov Monastery in Moscow. One hundred boyars were executed and many members of the middle class were deported with their families to Suzdal, north-east of Moscow.

Ivan had probably intended remaining in Novgorod to investigate the conspiracy further. It was at this time, however, that he learnt of the revolt of his brothers, Princes Andrei and Boris. Their main complaint was that Ivan had denied them a share of the estate of their other brother, Yury, and of the dominions annexed from Novgorod, which they had with their men helped him to conquer. Also Ivan had affronted his brothers, Prince Boris in particular, because contrary to his agreement he had sought to arrest Prince Ivan Obolensky-Lyko who had exercised his right to change his allegiance from Ivan to Boris, a right which Ivan did not admit and a defection which he would not accept.

Ivan arrived in Moscow from Novgorod on 13 February as the two brothers with their combined army of some 20,000 men moved westwards along the Volga River. Ivan sent envoys to persuade them to return, but the brothers rejected his urgent pleas and made their way to Velikie Luki. Here they were just inside the Muscovite frontier and conveniently placed to open negotiations with Casimir.

This revolt was for Ivan more than a domestic crisis; it threatened his whole policy and the very security of Muscovy. The defection of the two senior princes of the realm with an army of 20,000 would have been a major victory for Casimir. His Orthodox subjects would have been deeply impressed and their restless urge to defect to Moscow would have been calmed. The dangers of the revolt were the more acute because Ivan was receiving reports of a massive Tatar invasion, planned by Ahmad with the object of destroying Muscovy. In April Ivan sent Archbishop Vassian of Rostov to inform Andrei and Boris that if they returned to their patrimonies he would concede all their demands. But the brothers were waiting to see what terms Casimir would offer them and they rejected the proposals brought by Vassian. Soon, however, the position was reversed and they were sending messengers to Ivan and he was rejecting their offers. The reason for this change was that Casimir was not prepared to negotiate

with the two brothers or to help them. Deeply involved
with Khan Ahmad in seeking to mount joint campaigns
against Muscovy, Casimir may have felt that he needed
no further help. Whatever his reason, he rejected this
opportunity to weaken gravely the chief enemy of
Lithuania.

Ivan refused to accept the promises to swear allegiance which his brothers were now prepared to make.
He knew of the failure of their approaches to Casimir;
the Tatar invasion, expected in the summer, had been
far less serious than threatened and had been repelled;
he had just concluded his alliance with Mengli-Girei.
He was therefore in no hurry to treat with his brothers.

At this juncture the Livonians had invaded the republic of Pskov and laid siege to the city. In desperation the Pskovtsi had enlisted the help of the two
brothers, whose army was standing nearby around
Velikie Luki. But the Livonians had raised their siege
and withdrawn their forces before the brothers could
reach the city. The Pskovtsi, anxious not to incur the
anger of Ivan by conceding the demands made by
the two princes in return for their help, asked them
to withdraw, whereupon they ravaged extensive areas
of the republic. But the brothers with their large army
were now desperate to return to their patrimonies
and, indeed, they had nowhere else to go. At this
point the threat of a major invasion by the Golden
Horde had revived, and Ivan was prepared to negotiate with them. The terms finally agreed are not
known, but doubtless both sides made some concessions and in October [1480] Princes Andrei and Boris,
having sworn allegiance to their Grand Prince, returned to their principalities.

Ivan now turned again to Novgorod, determined
to eradicate treason from the city. A number of boyars
were interrogated and executed in the course of the

next four years. He then began deporting groups from the middle classes. In 1487 fifty prominent merchants were settled in Vladimir. The uncovering of a minor conspiracy among the middle class in the following year led to wholesale arrests. This time more than 7,000 Novgorod citizens were sent to Moscow. Some were executed, but the great majority were settled in Nizhni-Novgorod, Vladimir, Rostov, and elsewhere in the upper Volga–Oka region. Muscovite gentry and merchants, who were loyal to their Grand Prince and trustworthy, were then settled in Novgorod in their places.

By thus executing or resettling the boyars and most of the middle class Ivan had ensured that no actual or potential leaders remained to foment rebellions or weave conspiracies against his authority. The *veche* could no longer meet and its bell now hung in a belfry in Moscow. The patrimonial system of land tenure was abolished and the important frontier regions in the north-west and west were settled by Muscovites and others on service tenure. The Novgorod church ceased to be autonomous on the renunciation of his office by Archbishop Feofil in 1483. Novgorod had become a province of Muscovy.

Chapter Six

Pskov and Vyatka

TO the west of Novgorod lay the republic of Pskov. It covered a small area, some 200 miles long and 70 miles wide, running south from the Baltic and contained within the basin of the Velikaya River and Lake Chudskoe. The city of Pskov stood, strongly fortified, on the right bank of the Velikaya River and depended on the lakes and rivers for communications with other parts of the republic and for trade, especially to the north through Narva and the Baltic.

Dense forests and marshes covered much of the territory and, where cleared, the land was not very fertile, but was well cultivated. Rye, oats, and even wheat were grown, and flax of a high quality was the most important product of the soil. Around Pskov itself and other towns the people maintained small herds of dairy cattle and worked vegetable gardens. Fishing was also a valuable industry. Thus, unlike Novgorod, Pskov produced most of its own food and was not dependent on the import of supplies from its neighbours, except when the harvests failed, an occurrence which in the severity of the climate was not infrequent.

Another factor, distinguishing Pskov from the sister-republic of Novgorod, was the more even distribution of land and wealth among its citizens. It was a country of small-holdings, not of large estates, of artisans, and small traders. Crafts and industries, like boot and garment making, metal working for armour and weapons, and similar manufactures were highly developed, and trading in these and other goods was an important source of wealth. This absence of sharp distinctions between the very rich and very poor reduced friction and conflict among the people of Pskov, making them more aware of their common bonds. All felt, in rallying to the defence of the republic, that they were defending their own interests. The landowners and artisans themselves served and provided the troops who fought stoutly when Pskov was attacked, but less zealously when fighting away from their own lands for the Grand Prince of Moscow.

Pskov had been a province of Novgorod, administered, like Novgorod's other provinces, entirely by the governor and officials appointed for the purpose. Gradually, however, the people of Pskov had begun to govern themselves. They had learnt to be self-reliant in defending their own lands, whereas Novgorod was more taken up with developing its vast empire and accumulating wealth and had become dependent mainly on neighbours for protection. The defence of Pskov, as its westernmost territory, indeed became something of a burden for Novgorod, and in the 14th century the republic renounced its authority over Pskov. Thereafter the people of Pskov had elected their own governor and officials, and enjoyed the same autonomy and independence as their former master, except in the one respect that its church remained under the jurisdiction of the Novgorod Archbishop.

In electing its princes Pskov had turned sometimes to Lithuania and sometimes to Moscow. During the following century, however, it became the practice to elect the prince from Moscow or at least to obtain approval of its choice from the Grand Prince of Moscow. An important reason for this change was that in the first part of the 15th century Grand Prince Vitovt of Lithuania had sought to conquer the two republics and Pskov, like Novgorod, turning to Moscow for help, had naturally chosen Muscovite princes to serve as the head of the republic. In Pskov, moreover, the elected princes had gradually increased their authority and the *veche* had declined in importance. But, while unable to boast the same degree of independence as Novgorod, Pskov was still far from being a province of Muscovy, completely subject to the authority of the Grand Prince. Pskov was, in fact, bound by no treaty to assist Moscow in time of need, and the provision of troops from the republic and help of any kind always remained a matter of special negotiation.

More often, however, Pskov was compelled to seek the help of Moscow. In its exposed position to the west of Muscovy and Novgorod the republic frequently found itself the object of direct attacks. Along its western frontiers were the Teutonic Knights of Livonia and on its south-western frontier were the Lithuanians. Lakes, dense forests, and boglands provided natural defences against sudden invasions, and played an important part in Pskov's success in maintaining its independence for nearly 200 years. But for the people of the republic the price was constant struggle against their western enemies.

Livonia, embracing approximately the lands of the present-day Soviet Republics of Estonia and Latvia, was originally inhabited by Lithuanians and Letts. In the 12th century the Germans, mainly merchants and missionaries, came and many of the native population were converted to Christianity. In 1200 Bishop Albert had founded the city of Riga at the mouth of the Western Dvina. But then the Brotherhood of Sword-bearers, an order of crusading knights, subject to their own Grand Master, not to the Livonian Bishop, was established. Wearing a white cape marked with a red cross and with a sword on the shoulder, the knights were aggressive and acquisitive, and rapidly extended their power eastwards from Riga towards Pskov and the east Russian principalities of Polotsk and Smolensk. Another order, the Teutonic Order of Knights, occupied the lands between the Niemen and Vistula Rivers. This order, distinguished by a black cape with a white cross, had been formed to take part in the crusades of the Holy Land, but then in response to a Polish invitation to protect them, these knights had moved north into present-day Prussia. The two orders had subsequently amalgamated and in their drive eastwards had captured Pskov in 1241, but in the following year Alexander Nevsky on the frozen surface of Lake Chudskoe had routed them and recovered Pskov. Attacks by the Teutonic Knights had nevertheless continued and Pskov could never neglect its defences.

During the first half of the 15th century, however, the German knights were fairly inactive. Wealth and power had begun to sap their vigour and a process of decentralization of authority between the order and the bishops of the five chief cities of Livonia had weakened their leadership. Nevertheless about the middle of the century they had revived their eastward drive and begun preparing to invade Pskov and Novgorod. But the project had miscarried. Their plans to bring Denmark into the war had failed and their attempts to impose an economic blockade against Pskov and Novgorod had to be abandoned because of the hardships inflicted on their own towns. In 1448 they were glad to sign a fifteen-year peace with the two republics. War with Poland then absorbed their energies and it was not until 1480 that they again marched against Pskov.

To Ivan Pskov was a valuable defence outpost on

his north-western frontier. The republic was reliable and, unlike Novgorod, did not threaten to form alliances with his enemies. When towards the end of December 1470 he had sent envoys to Pskov, requesting troops to support him in his campaign against Novgorod, the *veche* had readily agreed. He had had to send two further envoys before the Pskov contingent was mobilized in July 1471. This delay was, however, clearly due to reluctance to send troops away from the republic, leaving it undefended even for a short time, and not to wavering loyalty. From long experience the Pskovtsi knew that the Livonian knights were always liable to attack.

During the late 1470s a number of incidents had suggested that the knights were preparing for war. Then in 1480 they made a sudden attack on the town of Vyshgorod to the south of Pskov and then hastily withdrew. In January of the following year the Livonians launched a stronger attack, this time on Gdov to the north of Pskov, and it was clear that this was the beginning of a major campaign, directed to the conquest of the republic.

Pskov appealed urgently for Muscovite help. Ivan was at this time in Novgorod and without delay sent an army, commanded by Prince Andrei Obolensky-Nogot, to defend the city. This Muscovite army as a reprisal at once invaded Livonia, laying waste the land as far as Dorpat. Obolensky then returned to Pskov but, instead of remaining to protect the republic, he suddenly led his army back into Muscovy. Learning of this withdrawal, the Master of the Order hurriedly mustered his forces and launched further invasions. The people of Pskov managed to ward off these attacks, but in doing so suffered heavy losses of life and severe damage to towns and villages.

Desperately Pskov sent messengers after Obolensky,

beseeching him to return to defend the republic. The appeals went unanswered. Ivan had recalled his army, because he himself was faced with a crisis, caused by the rebellion in February 1480 of his own brothers, Princes Andrei and Boris. The rebels had camped at Velikie Luki near the borders of Pskov and Lithuania and while they were in this region in August the Livonians suddenly invaded the republic of Pskov, attacking the fortress of Izborsk. They found that their attack made no impression on this stronghold and moved on to lay siege to Pskov itself. Again the city sent urgent appeals to Moscow and even to Novgorod to send troops. In desperation they begged help from the rebel princes who were so near at hand with their troops, some 20,000 strong, standing idle. At this point, and before Princes Andrei and Boris had arrived, the Livonians, losing all hope of taking the strongly fortified and stoutly defended city, raised their siege and retreated.

Early in September the two princes reached Pskov. There they were met with urgent requests that they should invade Livonia, leaving some troops to man the defences of Pskov against further attacks. But the princes made it a condition of their help that Pskov should assume full responsibility for their wives and children. This request faced the people of Pskov with the danger of incurring Moscow's wrath for giving refuge to the enemies of the Grand Prince and, unwilling to offend Ivan, they rejected the condition. Princes Andrei and Boris then withdrew their support and, venting their malice upon the republic, they sent their troops to ravage the land. "They laid waste many districts like infidels, and they plundered the houses of God and killed the cattle. They defiled the women and virgins and many they led off into captivity. Of all the animals they left not a chicken alive . . ." so the chronicler of Pskov recorded.

The next serious threat to Pskov came in 1501. The new Master of the Livonian Order, Von Plettenberg, had reached an agreement with Alexander, who had in June 1492 succeeded his father, Casimir, as Grand Prince of Lithuania, but not as King of Poland, for a joint Livonian–Lithuanian attack on Pskov and the surrounding lands. The intentions of these two western enemies were apparently known in Moscow, for the governor of Novgorod was alerted to have troops ready to go to the aid of Pskov. Tension mounted during the summer and in August a Muscovite army, commanded by Prince Daniil Penkov, arrived in Pskov. After some delay the Muscovite and Pskov armies marched and on 27 August they engaged the Livonians, led by their Master, on the Seritsa River to the south of Izborsk. The Russians quickly gained the upper hand, but then the Livonians brought up their artillery and put them to flight. The Master then tried to capture Izborsk, lying some twenty miles to the south-west of Pskov. Failing in this attempt he laid waste to the lands to the west of the Velikaya River, and early in September his troops, laden with plunder, withdrew into Livonia.

This Livonian invasion disturbed Ivan who at once mobilized a massive army to punish the knights and to secure the defences of this important outpost of his realm. He appointed Prince Daniil Shchenya, his most able and experienced general, in command of this great army, comprising troops from Moscow, Novgorod, Tver, and Pskov itself, and in November 1501 the Russians marched. At the fortress of Helmed near Dorpat, they came up with the main Livonian force, which they overwhelmed. Livonia then lay open to them. They laid waste extensive areas and plundered the region lying between Lakes Peipus [Chudskoe] and

Vorts. Some 40,000 Livonians are said to have been killed or taken captive. It was a swift retaliation for the Livonian invasion of Pskov and some years were to pass before the Master again dared to attack the republic.

Ivan had thus effectively demonstrated his readiness to defend Pskov against its enemies. But he took no steps to annex the city-republic or even to curtail its independence. Pskov posed no threat to his realm or to his policies. It was always a dependable ally and, since the republic needed Moscow's help against the Livonians, its loyalty to him and his heirs was fairly secure.

Vyatka was less dependable and was even a danger to Muscovy. This small republic embraced the upper reaches of the Vyatka River, to the north-east of Moscow and north of the Kazan Khanate, and had as its capital the town of Khlynov, a name by which the republic itself was sometimes known. Unlike Pskov whose people were predominantly traders, artisans, and peasants, the Vyatkans were wild, arrogant horsemen, more akin to the Tatars in their outlook and way of life. Vyatka had originally been founded as a colony of Novgorod, but in the 12th century had won its independence which the people guarded jealously. Towards the end of the 14th century the Tatars had conquered Vyatka and had compelled the people to pay tribute and acknowledge the suzerainty of the Khan. But the Vyatkans were too sturdy and belligerent to accept this status for long, and their subjection soon became no more than nominal. They conquered the Finnish tribes of the Votyaki and Cheremisi. When the Tatars threatened them they turned to Moscow for protection. When they found that the Grand Prince of Moscow also threatened their freedom, they promptly made alliances with the Khan. They were thus elusive, playing off their chief enemies against each other and always ready to raid and plunder and subdue their weaker neighbours.

To the Russians the Vyatkans were a constant source of trouble. They made periodic raids westwards into Muscovy and against Russian settlements to the north and north-west, and their raids were scarcely less destructive of life and property than the Tatar raids. But it was not their predatory invasions as much as their unreliability and the danger that they would join forces with the Tatars against Moscow that disturbed Ivan.

During the struggle for the throne of Moscow in 1451–52 between Vasily II and his cousin Dmitri Shemyaka, Vyatka had taken the side of Shemyaka and had actively supported him. After the defeat of Shemyaka, Vasily II had sent an expedition against the republic, probably as a reprisal. But in this first attempt his army had failed to conquer the republic. The second Muscovite expedition was successful, however, and in 1459 the Vyatkans were compelled to "bow submission to the Grand Prince according to his entire will, as is fitting to a sovereign". But as soon as the Muscovite army had departed, the people of Vyatka, showing that they were far from subjugated, reclaimed their independence, and preoccupied elsewhere, the Grand Prince apparently made no immediate attempts to re-enforce his authority.

In 1468, when preparing for a campaign against the Khanate of Kazan, Ivan III sent couriers to Vyatka calling on the people to provide troops in support of his armies. The Vyatkans not only refused troops, but declared their neutrality in the impending war. Three years later, however, they made some amends by supporting his campaign to subdue Novgorod. The Vyatkans had nursed a deep hostility towards Novgorod since the time when Vyatka had been a colony. But they soon demonstrated their independence anew when in 1486 they raided the Muscovite province of Ustyug in the north-west. In the following year they again refused to send their troops against Kazan. This time Ivan appealed to their religious faith. Metropolitan Gerontii at his request called upon the Vyatkans to oppose the Muslim Tatars and not to commit the sin of helping them against their fellow Christians. He even threatened them with excommunication. The Vyatkans made no reply and Ivan decided now on military action. In 1489 he sent a strong army, commanded by his two leading generals, Prince Daniil Shchenya and Boyar Grigori Morozov, and supported by troops from Ustyug and the North Dvina regions where the people had suffered from the invasions of the Vyatkans and were eager for revenge. The Muscovite army arrived before Khlynov on 16 August 1489 and the commanders called on the Vyatkans to surrender three of their leaders and to swear loyalty to the Grand Prince. For three days the Vyatkans hesitated and then they submitted.

Ivan was now determined to put an end to the dangers to which the republic constantly exposed him. He ordered that all the citizens of Vyatka with their families should be brought to the Moscow region. He had their three leaders executed in Moscow and the people were enlisted in his service, some being granted estates on service tenure. But all were moved far from their homeland and in their place he settled loyal citizens from Muscovy.

This policy of the resettlement of several thousand people which he had also applied in Novgorod was particularly effective in Vyatka. By this means he dealt with a serious danger to the security of his eastern frontier and in its place created a stronghold against the Tatars. At this time, moreover, he needed to reinforce his frontiers and to secure the country as far as possible against attacks in the east, so that he would be free to pursue his plans against Lithuania.

Chapter Seven

Diplomatic Relations with the West

THE last quarter of the 15th century witnessed a marked increase in Muscovite diplomatic relations with Western Europe. Contact with the West had hitherto been slight and infrequent, the most important exchange having been with Rome in 1469–72 concerning the marriage with Zoe Palaeologa. The chief reason for Muscovy's isolation had been the long period of Tatar domination and also her insignificance and the fact that she had been cut off from her Western neighbours by the extensive territories of Novgorod and by the independent principalities of Tver and Ryazan. It was only after Ivan had annexed them that Muscovy acquired a common frontier with Lithuania. By this time, moreover, Tatar power had crumbled and the power of Moscow had grown greatly. Lithuania and Livonia had begun to fear her, but others in the West also sought to make use of her against their own enemies, and this was the reason for their approaches.

Diplomatic exchanges with Moscow were, however, hindered by the long and hazardous journeys which envoys had to make. Months passed while embassies travelled by roundabout routes, bearing messages which had been overtaken by events or proposals which were no longer practicable by the time they reached their destinations. Nevertheless during this period Ivan and certain Western rulers persevered in their efforts to exchange envoys and negotiate alliances.

It was noteworthy that the diplomatic approaches were first made to Ivan in each case and they bore witness to the new prestige and power of Moscow, which only a few decades earlier had been a minor principality, one among several in north-eastern Russia. Ivan welcomed all such approaches. He rejected no proposals until he was sure that they would not serve his policy. At the same time he took care to extract other benefits from these exchanges, as, for example, when he charged his envoys to engage foreign technicians, engineers, and architects for service in Russia. But the touchstone was whether a proposal could further his plans against Lithuania. This had been the reason for his patient pursuit of an understanding with the Crimean Khan, Mengli-Girei, which had resulted in 1480 in their offensive alliance against Lithuania. It was the prime reason also for his keen interest in the three diplomatic approaches made to him at this time—from Moldavia, Hungary, and the Holy Roman Empire—for all were concerned with alliances against Poland-Lithuania.

Moldavia, comprising the present-day Moldavian Republic and a part of eastern Roumania, was threatened on all sides. Her most dangerous enemy was the Ottoman Porte whose Sultan was determined to control the shores of the Black Sea and especially the mouth of the Danube as the first step to domination of the Danubian lands. But Poland in the north and Hungary to the west also coveted her territory. In fact, Moldavia would, like Serbia and Bulgaria, have been conquered long before this time had it not been for the ability and courage of her ruler, Stephen IV, the Great, who warded off the Turks and the Tatars and his other enemies for nearly fifty years. In 1476, however, Sultan Mohammed II, the Conqueror, invaded Moldavia and defeated Stephen, who was saved only by a Hungarian army which forced the Turks to retreat.

At this time Stephen was desperately seeking new allies. Wallachia, Hungary, and Poland were engaged elsewhere and were unwilling to become involved in the defence of Moldavia. The Pope and the western countries to whom he had appealed earlier for help had not responded. There remained Muscovy and Stephen could not be sure of Muscovite support. Ivan wanted no trouble with the Turks at this time, when he was preparing to attack Lithuania. He had, in fact, tried without success to make a treaty of friendship with the Sultan to secure himself from Turkish invasions while he was engaged in the north. Moreover, he was counting heavily on his alliance with Mengli-Girei, the Crimean Khan, who was now the Sultan's vassal, and this was a further reason why he could not antagonize the Turks.

Stephen decided nevertheless the seek closer understanding with Ivan through the marriage of his daughter, Elena, with Ivan's son, Ivan Molodoi. Ivan welcomed the proposal, having evidently satisfied himself that this would not compromise him in the eyes of the Turks, and after some delay Elena and Ivan Molodoi were married in Moscow on 1 January 1483. In the course of the marriage negotiations Ivan and Stephen probably reached some agreement to help each other against Casimir, then ruler of Poland and Lithuania, but it would seem that Ivan made it clear that he would not aid Stephen against Turkey.

In July–August 1484 Bayazit II, the "Saint-Sultan" who had succeeded on the death of his father, Mohammed II, three years earlier, captured Moldavia's two most important Black Sea ports, Kilia at the mouth of the Danube, and Cetatea Alba [Belgorod] at the mouth of the Dniester. The fact that the Sultan referred to Kilia as the key and gateway to Moldavia and Hungary, and to Cetatea Alba as the key and gateway to Poland, Russia, and Tataria was evidence of his intentions. But Ivan concentrated on his plans against Lithuania and was not drawn into any agreement to help Stephen against the Turks. Indeed, during the years following the Turkish conquest Ivan and Stephen apparently had no contact, although it was a time when Moldavia was desperately in need of allies. But after 1488 they exchanged numerous messages which presumably concerned a coalition against Casimir.

In 1492 Ivan learnt from Mengli-Girei that his Khanate was now allied with Moldavia against Poland–Lithuania. In the following year the news reached Moscow that Stephen had twice invaded Polish territory and, surprisingly, that he had allowed Turkish troops to march through Moldavia to attack Poland. This was the kind of support that Ivan needed, for no matter how minor the attacks, they diverted the troops and devastated the lands of his enemies.

Thus, while the Crimean Tatars made frequent invasions north into the Dnieper region, then belonging to Lithuania, Moldavian forces laid waste the Podolia, belonging to Poland, advancing as far north as Lvov. Casimir, as King of Poland and Grand Prince of Lithuania, was constantly distracted. He was obliged to keep troops ready to repel attacks along an extensive frontier. All the time his great enemy, Ivan, while encouraging this pressure from the south, was fomenting border warfare against Lithuania, and preparing for the day when Muscovite armies would mount a full-scale invasion to recover the lands which belonged to his patrimony.

An approach by Matthias Corvinus, King of Hungary, proposing an alliance against Poland, delighted Ivan at this time. Under the rule of Matthias, who was an able soldier and ruler, Hungary was a strong state, well placed to invade and inflict serious damage on the Poles. Ivan responded at once by sending one of his leading counsellors, the secretary [*dyak*] Feodor Kuritsyn, with detailed proposals for an offensive alliance against Poland–Lithuania, which Matthias promptly accepted. Kuritsyn was, however, seriously delayed on his return from Hungary and did not reach Moscow until over two years later.

This return journey illustrated clearly the kinds of delays and hazards which faced envoys at this time, in addition to the vast distances which they had to cover. Leaving Buda, Kuritsyn avoided Polish and Lithuanian territory and travelled by way of Moldavia. He reached Belgorod in 1484 shortly after Sultan Bayazit had captured the town. The Turks at once imprisoned him and his party and only released them several months later on the appeal of Matthias. The Turks then handed over the Russians to the Crimean Khan who sent them on to Moscow.

Confusion and suspicion arose from these delays. Matthias sent an envoy to Ivan, urging him not to make peace with Casimir. But Ivan was still impatiently awaiting the arrival of Kuritsyn, who was bringing the formal confirmation of the Russo-Hungarian alliance against Poland. Deeply cautious by nature, he could not be sure that the Hungarian King was an ally until he had the formal treaty in his hand.

In July 1488 Ivan sent messages with the returning Hungarian envoy, urging Matthias to attack Poland.

At the same time he despatched to Hungary by way of the Crimea and Moldavia his own envoy charged with the task of impressing on Matthias the need to invade Poland without delay. By this time, however, Ivan had come to believe that Matthias had no real intention of marching against their common enemy. But he may well have been wrong in this suspicion. If communications had been speedier between the two rulers, some joint action might well have resulted. In 1490, however, Matthias died. Vladislav of Bohemia, who succeeded him, united Bohemia and Hungary and forged a strong alliance between them and Poland–Lithuania. The proposed alliance between Muscovy and Hungary thus proved abortive. The one benefit which Ivan derived from it was the engagement of a number of engineers and architects, mainly Italians, to help in the work of rebuilding Moscow.

Negotiations with the Holy Roman Empire proved equally unprofitable. Again the first approach was made to Ivan. Emperor Frederick III [1440–93] in the course of a reign of disasters was sustained by a fervent belief in Habsburg destiny. His empire was rent by warring rulers, many of whom had established themselves independently of him. By the early 1480s he was alarmed by the danger that Poland–Lithuania, Bohemia, and Hungary would be joined in an effective alliance against him, and indeed this coalition was to come into existence in the following decade. Concerned with the reassertion of imperial power in Eastern Europe and especially with the recovery of lower Austria with Vienna which Matthias had conquered, and with establishing power over Hungary, coveted by Casimir, the Emperor sought new allies. He had heard vague reports of the might of the emerging nation to the north-east and considered that with such an ally he would be able to deal with Casimir. But first the Emperor sent Nikolaus Poppel informally to Moscow to make a first-hand investigation of Muscovite strength and to report on the authority and position of the Grand Prince. In particular Poppel was to ascertain whether Ivan was, in fact, dependent on Casimir, a belief which demonstrated the ignorance about Russia then common in Western Europe.

Unaccustomed to informal envoys who came not in full dignity but privately and merely with a letter of recommendation, Ivan and his court were reserved in their treatment of Poppel, suspecting him of being a Polish spy, and they placed many difficulties in his way. Nevertheless, on his return from Moscow Poppel impressed the Emperor with his report that Ivan was not only an independent sovereign, and in no sense a vassal, but that he possessed far greater wealth and armed might than Casimir. Without delay Frederick sent Poppel back to Moscow, this time as his fully accredited ambassador. Again Poppel aroused Muscovite suspicions. He boasted overmuch of enjoying the Emperor's confidence and friendship. He surrounded himself with secrecy and was disastrously ignorant of the protocol which played a part of real importance at the court of Moscow.

Poppel brought two proposals from the Emperor. The first was that Ivan should marry one of his daughters to the Emperor's nephew, the Margrave of Baden. The second proposal was hedged with mystery by Poppel who revealed it only in private audience. This was that Ivan should take advantage of the Emperor's goodwill to obtain from him the title of king. The proposal was both tactless and offensive to Ivan and it drew from him the firm and dignified reply, quoted on page 40 above, that his appointment was from God and that he required no other.

On this note Poppel's mission closed. Ivan was, however, anxious to follow up the Emperor's initiative, particularly as Frederick was the enemy of Casimir. In March 1489 he sent Yury Trakhaniot, a member of Sofia's court and an able man, to express his earnest desire for friendship with the Emperor. Yury Trakhaniot was received in Frankfurt by the Emperor's son, Maximilian, who possessed his father's talent for evasive diplomacy and who had been elected King of Rome in 1486. To him Yury conveyed Ivan's rejection of the marriage proposal, making it clear that the daughter of the Muscovite Grand Prince could not marry a lowly Margrave. He also requested permission to enlist goldsmiths and gunsmiths, engineers and artisans to serve in Muscovy. It was this task of engaging experts which probably accounted for the six-month delay in his return to Moscow, but it was apparently all that was gained by his mission.

Events were, however, moving rapidly in Eastern Europe. Matthias, King of Hungary, was determined that his bastard son, John Corvinus, should succeed him. This meant negotiating a revocation of the treaty of 1463, providing that the Emperor, Frederick, or his successor, should ascend the Hungarian throne on the death of Matthias. Maximilian now expressed himself ready to guarantee the succession of John Corvinus in return for the surrender of Austria and the frontier town of Pressburg [Bratislava]. But on 6 April 1490 Matthias died before agreement on these terms could be reached.

Two months before the death of Matthias, however, the imperial ambassador, von Thurn, had set out for Moscow, accompanied by the returning

Russian envoy. Von Thurn bore the proposal that Ivan should attack Poland–Lithuania in the event of Vladislav or another of Casimir's sons opposing Maximilian in his plans to recover Hungary by arms or by peaceful methods. The explanation of the apparent conflict in imperial policy towards Hungary may have been that, while Frederick had no intention of surrendering his claims to the Hungarian throne, his son, Maximilian, was prepared to negotiate an exchange of the throne for the Austrian lands. Von Thurn on his arrival in Moscow even proposed that Ivan should send Muscovite troops to serve in Flanders against Maximilian's enemy, the King of France. In return for this military aid, Ivan was merely offered the marriage of one of his daughters to Maximilian who, as it transpired, had already agreed to a more advantageous marriage elsewhere.

Ivan was very guarded in his reply to these one-sided propositions. He agreed to the marriage, subject to his daughter being guaranteed complete freedom of worship according to the Orthodox faith. He was also prepared to form an alliance with the Emperor, but on terms to be dictated by him in Moscow. The treaty which he proposed was hedged with conditions and bound him to render military aid only in the event that Maximilian was actively engaged in recovering Hungary, and Maximilian was to give him similar help when he marched to recover Kiev.

At this time Ivan did not know that Matthias had died or that Maximilian had marched and was on the point of taking Vienna. Nor did he know that Casimir's son, Vladislav II of Bohemia, had already been crowned King of Hungary. Maximilian had, in fact, captured Vienna in August [1490] and was advancing into Hungary in November, when a mutiny among his troops and lack of funds halted him. He was in Nürnberg desperately trying to raise money to continue his Hungarian campaign and his struggle against Charles VIII of France, when von Thurn and the Russian ambassador arrived from Moscow.

Maximilian readily agreed the treaty proposed by Ivan. He was then actively engaged in recovering Hungary and the treaty therefore obliged Ivan to go to his aid. But Maximilian had probably come to realize at this stage that his Hungarian campaign was doomed to failure. Moreover, he was anxious to concentrate on his struggle against France for possession of Britanny. He therefore proposed an ambitious, somewhat impractical northern alliance, comprising the Livonians, the Prussian towns, and Muscovy, all under the leadership of Ivan, which would keep Poland–Lithuania in check in the north. Stephen of Moldavia and the Crimean Khan would attack from the south. Maximilian was also planning to secure the Swedish throne. Threatened on so many sides, Casimir and Vladislav would, he believed, release their hold on Hungary, which would fall into his hands, while he would all the time be free to give his full attention to his struggle against France.

Ivan was not impressed by these plans which von Thurn on his arrival in Moscow in November 1491 submitted to him. Moreover, he had learnt before granting the German ambassador his first audience that on 7 November 1491 the Treaty of Pressburg had been signed. By this treaty Maximilian had recognized Vladislav of Bohemia as King of Hungary, and had received in return the cession of the Austrian provinces and the right for himself and his heirs of succession to the Hungarian throne in the event of Vladislav dying without heir.

Maximilian had thus given up his struggle for Hungary and certainly could not claim Ivan's help under their treaty of alliance. Nor was Ivan prepared to support the grandiose scheme for a northern alliance or the claim to the Swedish throne. At the same time, while disappointed in Maximilian, Ivan did not denounce the treaty or break off negotiations while he saw even the smallest chance of an effective alliance against Poland–Lithuania.

In May 1492 Ivan sent Yury Trakhaniot in charge of another embassy to Maximilian. He instructed him to gather information and to report on Maximilian's position and intentions not only in Austria and Hungary, but also in Brittany and France. The embassy sent him several reports en route, and Trakhaniot made it abundantly clear that Maximilian, having become Vladislav's ally by the Treaty of Pressburg, was no longer interested in an alliance with Ivan, and would certainly not help him against Lithuania, despite his agreement to do so.

Maximilian received the envoys in audience in January 1493. He skilfully avoided answering their questions and countered with proposals for a grand alliance against the Ottoman Porte. He even made the suggestion, totally unacceptable to the Russians, that they should travel to Breslau to discuss this crusade with Vladislav, who was already King of Bohemia and Hungary, and with Jan Olbracht, King of Poland, and Alexander, Grand Prince of Lithuania, the sons of Casimir who had succeeded after his death on 7 June 1492. The Russian embassy returned to Moscow and during the rest of Ivan's reign no further exchanges took place with Maximilian.

Ivan had throughout these diplomatic negotiations with Moldavia, Hungary, and the Empire shown himself to be subtle and tenacious. He did not at any time lose sight of his own objectives. He gained experience and information of Western courts, and from Stephen of Moldavia he had valuable support against Poland–Lithuania. His negotiations with Matthias of Hungary and with Frederick and Maximilian yielded nothing apart from the opportunity to enlist Western technicians. But it was not through any failure on his part that the exchanges were not more fruitful.

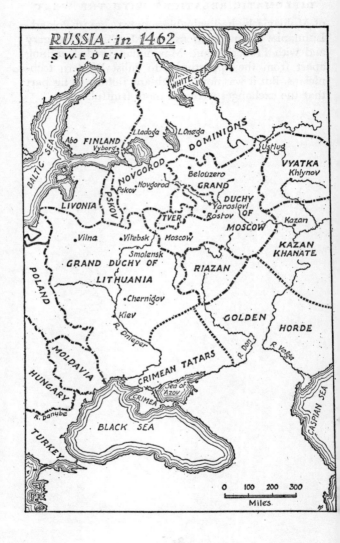

RUSSIA in 1462

SWEDEN

WHITE SEA

BALTIC SEA

Abo FINLAND
Vyborg

L.Ladoga   L.Onega

DOMINIONS

Ustiug

VYATKA
Khlynov

NOVGOROD
Pskov   Novgorod

Belouzero

GRAND
DUCHY
OF
MOSCOW

LIVONIA

PSKOV

TVER

Yaroslavl
Rostov

Kazan

Vilna   Vitebsk   Moscow

Smolensk

GRAND DUCHY OF

KAZAN
KHANATE

LITHUANIA

RIAZAN

Chernigov

Kiev

R. Dnieper

GOLDEN

HORDE

POLAND

R. Don

R. Volga

MOLDAVIA

HUNGARY

CRIMEAN TATARS

Sea of
Azov

R. Danube

CRIMEA

CASPIAN SEA

TURKEY

BLACK SEA

0   100   200   300
Miles.

Chapter Eight

Ivan's Lithuanian Campaign Begins

IVAN'S reign has been described as a careful, systematic preparation for the Russo–Lithuanian War of 1500–03 in which he achieved nearly all that he sought. But historians, looking back over the centuries, are often prone to discover a pattern which they can attribute to the masterly planning of one man, and they overlook the factors of expediency and accident, which were all-important at the time. Thus, while acknowledging the vision, singlemindedness, and ability of Ivan, it is necessary also to recognize that the pattern which his reign reveals was due not to his masterly planning so much as his tenacity in pursuing his objectives and his ability to seize on events and turn them to his advantage.

Ivan's determination to unite all Russia under the rule of Moscow had made war against Lithuania unavoidable. In the previous century the Grand Princes of Lithuania had annexed and still retained most of west and south-west Russia and of the Ukraine, all of which Ivan considered to be part of his patrimony. His first task, on succeeding to the throne, had been to establish his authority in north-eastern Russia and to secure his eastern and southern frontiers against attack. He had then begun his struggle against Lithuania. He was not at once prepared to go to war and in any case he regarded war as a gamble to be taken only when there was no alternative and the odds were heavily in his favour. But by a process of frontier attacks and subversion he took the initiative and made substantial gains.

The border warfare which marked the first stage of Ivan's campaign probably began in earnest in 1478. In that year he asserted his sovereignty over Novgorod and this gave Muscovy a common frontier with Lithuania for the first time. Along this frontier Muscovite attacks on Lithuanian lands and subjects increased in intensity during the next ten years, reaching a climax in 1487–89. Whether they were part of an organized campaign or whether they amounted to a series of independent actions will never be known with certainty. Following Tatar tactics, bands of Muscovites made lightning raids over the border, burning villages, plundering, and driving the people and livestock back into Muscovy. Because so swift, frequent, and unexpected, these raids were demoralizing to the people of eastern Lithuania. Moreover, since the majority of them were Orthodox Russians, they were more readily persuaded to transfer their allegiance to Moscow by such tactics. But sometimes in this warfare large forces advanced across the frontier in what were major invasions, and these expeditions resulted in the capture of hundreds of prisoners and often in the virtual annexation of Lithuanian territory. Thus the campaigns were probably a combination of independent raids and large-scale invasions, the former spontaneous movements, the latter organized military operations. Ivan undoubtedly encouraged aggression against Lithuania at this time and probably gave orders for the major operations. But in his replies to Casimir's protests he always indignantly denied all knowledge and responsibility.

Ivan's purpose in encouraging and indeed in organizing these operations was twofold. First, such acts of aggression gave him the initiative and the moral advantage which came from forcing the Lithuanians on to the defensive. They made desperate counterattacks as Muscovite pressure mounted, but the initiative remained with Ivan, and increasingly the Lithuanians felt awed by the power of Muscovy. Second, the border warfare made a strong impact on the Orthodox Russian princes and boyars, whose lands were situated in eastern Lithuania. Many of them were induced to transfer their allegiance to Moscow and to join with their fellow Russians and co-religionists against the Lithuanian enemy. They may have reasoned also that since Casimir could not protect them against this constant aggression they would be more secure under the wing of Ivan. Moreover, when they defected to Moscow, they often brought with them their estates, their armed bands, and their peasants. In fact, the defection of princes and boyars with their estates amounted in some regions to moving the Muscovite frontier farther to the west.

The border lands over which this warfare raged for more than ten years extended from the Velikie Luki enclave, just south of the city-republic of Pskov, down to the region of the upper Oka River. Velikie Luki and also Rzhev were in Muscovite hands, but Casimir claimed some rights in both places, which Ivan refused to consider. The other towns and districts, possession of which was disputed, were on the Lithuanian side of the border. The Toropets district had formerly been held jointly by Lithuania and Novgorod before Ivan's annexation of the latter in 1478, and this gave substance to Ivan's claim to it. To the south-east lay the hereditary lands of the Belsky, centred on the town of Bely on the Obsha River. In 1481 Prince Feodor I.

Belsky transferred his allegiance to Moscow and he was to play an important part in the warfare in this region. Farther to the south-east was the principality of Vyazma, centred on the town and river of the same name. Then came a number of small principalities in the upper Oka area over which Lithuania's authority was uncertain.

The extensive frontier region fell into three sectors and may well have been divided into three commands. The Toropets region apparently came under the command of Prince Feodor Belsky. Responsibility for subduing Vyazma was shared between Ivan's brother, Prince Andrei, and his son, Ivan Molodoi, who maintained a steady pressure of attacks on the whole principality. In the third sector, embracing the north-western part of the upper Volga region, the governor of Medyn, Prince Vasily Pestry, was in command, but the most active commanders were Ivan, Vasily, and Peter S. Odoevsky and Prince Ivan Vorotynsky-Peremyshlsky, all of whom had sworn allegiance to Ivan some years earlier. They had continued to hold their hereditary estates, although on the Lithuanian side of the frontier, and used them as bases from which to attack neighbouring lands.

The pro-Muscovite princes persuaded and coerced their relatives and neighbours into swearing allegiance to Moscow. The Odoevsky brothers used force to compel their cousin, Prince Feodor I. Odoevsky, to follow their suit. Prince Feodor I. Vorotynsky annexed his brother's share of their patrimony and made all his boyars and servitors swear allegiance to Ivan. Throughout the troubled frontier lands princes and boyars who felt no strong allegiance to Casimir, but had no wish to defect to Ivan, found themselves under similar heavy pressure. In increasing numbers, whether voluntarily or involuntarily, they transferred their allegiance to

Moscow. Casimir sent protests to Ivan, who denied all responsibility or in some cases claimed that the defecting princes were merely acknowledging their rightful sovereign. He also countered with complaints about the treatment of his merchants in Lithuania.

In May 1492 Ivan sent a certain Ivan Bersen-Beklemishev with replies to Casimir's various protests and also with numerous demands and complaints of his own. Ivan's instructions to Bersen showed that at this stage he claimed only the northern part of the principality of Vyazma. But it was also clear that he had no intention of surrendering the extensive estates, transferred to Moscow by the owners changing their allegiance. In short, Ivan was moderate in merely requiring Casimir to accept the status quo. He was achieving his purposes by a steady process of attrition, and he had no desire to disturb the process by presenting exorbitant demands. Bersen had no opportunity to submit Ivan's complaints and demands, however, for on the road to Lithuania he learnt that Casimir had died on 7 June [1492], and he at once returned to Moscow.

Casimir had been King of Poland and Grand Prince of Lithuania, but on his death one son, Jan Olbracht, succeeded to the Polish throne, while another son, Alexander, became Grand Prince of Lithuania. Many among the Lithuanian nobles, while gratified that the principality now had a separate and independent prince, were disturbed by the succession of Alexander. He was not lacking in ability or in strength of character, but he was young and showed little promise of becoming the vigorous and dominating ruler that his father had been. The Lithuanians' misgivings were all the more pressing because they were alarmed by the mounting pressure of Muscovite aggression along their frontier and the piecemeal annexation of their territory. They realized that they could not halt this movement by arms, for the might of Muscovy was already greater than that of Lithuania. The solution decided on was to induce Ivan to agree to the marriage of his daughter to Grand Prince Alexander. Such a dynastic marriage seemed the only possible way to persuade Ivan to call off hostilities.

The death of Casimir had been followed by a fury of Muscovite attacks. Ivan was apparently taking advantage of falling Lithuanian morale and of the youthful inexperience of Alexander. In August 1492 the princes of Odoev and Peremyshl destroyed Mosalsk, taking all the local princes captive. In the upper Oka region increased pressure was brought to bear on the princes who had not yet sworn allegiance to Ivan, and Muscovite troops occupied part of the principality of Vyazma. Towards the end of 1492 Prince Semeon Vorotynsky, having suffered the abduction of his retainers and the devastation of his estates, finally swore allegiance to Ivan. Early in 1493 Muscovite troops took the important towns of Serpeisk and Meshchovsk. Prince Mikhail Romanovich of Meshchovsk had already defected to Moscow, taking his two brothers, Semeon and Peter, with him by force. Ivan rewarded him with the grant of the entire Meshchovsk principality. The conquest of the principality of Vyazma crowned the Muscovite campaign in the winter of 1492–93. Ivan had appointed Prince Daniil Shchenya and Prince Vasily Patrikeev, two of his most able commanders, to conduct this operation. But the princes and people of Vyazma apparently offered little resistance and readily accepted the Grand Prince of Moscow as their sovereign. Ivan at once restored their patrimonial estates to the princes, but on the condition that they served him loyally.

Meanwhile the Lithuanian nobles had made their

first approaches to Moscow. Only a few weeks after Casimir's death, Zaberezinsky, the governor of Polotsk, and Nicholas Radziwill, *voevoda* of Vilna and Chancellor of Lithuania, sent private messages to Yakov Zakharin, the governor of Novgorod, and to Ivan Patrikeev, the senior boyar at Ivan's court. They proposed a peace treaty and marriage between their Grand Prince and Ivan's daughter. They promised to bring all persuasion to bear on Alexander, if Zakharin and Patrikeev would induce Ivan to accept these propositions.

Ivan warmly welcomed this approach. He saw the opportunity to negotiate a treaty, formally acknowledging his territorial gains. He also saw many advantages in the proposed marriage. But he was careful to mask his pleasure and to curb his impatience to begin negotiations. At this time the conquest of Vyazma and of the Serpeisk–Meshchovsk region had still to be effected and possession of these lands would enable him to negotiate from greater strength.

The private Lithuanian–Muscovite exchanges continued from July to October 1492. In November two Lithuanian envoys arrived in Moscow to make the usual formal complaints about Muscovite attacks, but they also enquired informally whether Ivan favoured a peace treaty and marriage. Still displaying no enthusiasm, Ivan let it be known that both treaty and marriage were desirable.

Not only was Ivan waiting on further conquests of Lithuanian territory before beginning negotiations, but also he was troubled during the winter of 1492–93 by what may have been a dangerous plot to murder him. Details of the conspiracy are scanty. Evidently it centred on a minor Lithuanian prince, Ivan Lukomsky, sent by Casimir to join Ivan's service and to poison him on a suitable opportunity. After close interrogation

Lukomsky was imprisoned in an iron cage on the frozen Moskva River, and there burnt to death. Others implicated in the plot were flogged to death or executed.

In January 1493 Ivan took a step which might well have jeopardized the negotiations for a peace treaty, but which demonstrated clearly the ascendancy which he felt over the Lithuanians. His envoy, despatched to carry the complaints and counter-complaints which he regularly exchanged with the Grand Prince of Lithuania, was instructed to speak in the name of "Ioann, by the grace of God, Sovereign of all Russia and Grand Prince . . ." He had never before used this full title in his diplomatic missions, but had merely called himself "Grand Prince". It was a major change in tradition and protocol, which in the 15th century could lead to endless disputes and even to the breaking-off of diplomatic relations and to war. Moreover, the title of "Sovereign of all Russia" was clear warning to Alexander that he formally claimed all Russian territory, which included vast areas forming part of the Lithuanian realm.

Alexander was on the defensive and desperate to gain as long a respite as possible from Muscovite attacks. He had tried to obtain troops and money from Poland for a campaign against Muscovy, but without success. He had raised objections to Ivan's new titles, but had met with the stubborn assertions that these titles were from God and not to be disputed. He had delayed embarking on negotiations for a treaty with Ivan, probably hoping still that some help might come from Poland. Finally his ambassadors were briefed in Vilna in November 1493 and they arrived in Moscow in the following January.

At their first audience the Lithuanian ambassadors presented Alexander's demand that the frontier should be settled as it had been in 1449. This meant that all subsequent Russian acquisitions should be surrendered. The Russian representatives, Prince Vasily Patrikeev and Semeon Ryapolovsky, then proposed that the frontier should be restored to the position held before the original Lithuanian conquests. But these were merely the opening gambits, the preliminary skirmishes, which were a formal part of all such diplomatic engagements, and they were not seriously intended by either party. The ambassadors then put forward realistic claims and proposals. The negotiations quickly developed into a bitter struggle in which the Lithuanians were compelled to give ground. First, they agreed to surrender all claims to Vyazma. This was the demand to which Ivan attached most importance at this stage, for Vyazma would give him a sound foothold from which to attack Smolensk. In the further discussions over the other disputed, but less important, territories, Ivan displayed a wise magnanimity. He conceded Alexander's rights to Dmitrov, Mosalsk, Mtsensk, and Lyubutsk, and even to the Meshchovsk sectors which his troops had seized. Furthermore he agreed to allow Princes Semeon and Peter Romanovich, who had been forcibly brought to Moscow by their brother, Prince Mikhail, to decide freely whether they would serve him or Alexander.

Ivan's concessions cleared the way for prompt agreement of the treaty and he was gratified by his gains. In its moderation it illustrated Ivan's practice of gradual, but remorseless, achievement of his goals. He had at this stage merely won recognition of his possession of certain of the regions and towns which were in his hands, while Lithuania yielded nothing that she actually held at the time. But Ivan saw this treaty merely as the first step in his campaign, and in this light his gains were considerable. First, he had confirmed the acceptance of his title as "Ioann, by the grace of God, Sovereign of all Russia" to which he attached great importance. He had gained the strategically invaluable principality of Vyazma from which he could move against Smolensk, the key to the conquest of the north-western lands. He had strengthened his position in the upper Volga region, from which in due course his armies could advance westwards.

The Muscovite representatives, Patrikeev and Ryapolovsky, now indicated that they were ready to discuss the marriage between Grand Prince Alexander and Ivan's daughter, Elena. At the outset they demanded that Elena must be guaranteed freedom of worship in her Orthodox faith and that this freedom should not be limited in any way. The Lithuanian ambassadors at once agreed and on the following day, in the presence of Grand Princess Sofia. Elena was betrothed to Alexander, who was represented by a proxy. But now Ivan insisted on a deed, to be signed by Alexander, formally swearing that Elena would in no way be harmed in her faith. This was an indication both of Muscovite fear and suspicion of Roman Catholic subversion and persecution, but also it suggested that Ivan already had it in mind to make an issue, and indeed a *casus belli* of his daughter's freedom of worship.

The deed, as dictated by Ivan, was taken to Vilna to be signed under oath. Alexander insisted, however, on adding a further clause that if Elena "wishes of her own accord to join in our Roman faith, then she shall have freedom to do this". The Muscovite ambassadors refused to accept the additional words. Ivan, when this was reported to him, made no comment and took no action, merely waiting, confident that Alexander would not press the matter to the point of endangering the marriage and the treaty. In August Lithuanian ambassadors arrived in Moscow to discuss the new clause, but were bluntly told that there would be no marriage, unless the deed, as dictated by Ivan, was executed. Alexander duly signed it as required.

In January 1495 a formal Lithuanian embassy arrived in Moscow to conduct the bride to their Grand Prince in Vilna. At this late stage Ivan briefed his daughter verbally and in writing on the attitude she was to take towards the Roman Church. His instructions were exhaustive and petty. Moreover, he appointed a suite, eighty strong, to accompany her and remain with her in Lithuania. To the princes, senior boyars, and churchmen of this suite, he gave further detailed instructions concerning protocol and the procedures to be observed during the marriage ceremony and on all occasions in which the Roman Church was involved. The progress of Elena to Vilna and her wedding were marred by countless incidents when Orthodox priests and members of her suite crudely intervened. The Lithuanians were incensed, but they dared not risk provoking the Muscovites.

The reason for Ivan's exaggerated concern for Elena's Orthodoxy can only be surmised. Ivan himself, although a member of the Orthodox church, was not bigoted. His dominant interest was politics and the achievement of his political objectives. He readily negotiated with Moslems, Roman Catholics, and Protestants, and his closest ally, Mengli-Girei, was a Moslem. Later he was to show tolerance towards heretical sects in his own country. Thus, not religious fanaticism, but political strategy, was at the root of his reiterated concern for his daughter's faith.

The marriage of Elena with Alexander was, in fact, typical of Ivan's ruthless methods. He did not hesitate to swear to maintain peace and friendship with Alexander, while regarding their treaty of peace as merely the first stage in his campaign against Lithuania. He did not hesitate to sacrifice his own daughter to the same cause. He considered that the presence of the Orthodox Princess in Vilna would help rally Alexander's many Russian Orthodox subjects to the Muscovite side. On the other hand, if Elena were to succumb to the subversion of Roman Catholic priests, it would severely damage Muscovite and Orthodox prestige. At the same time he intended that Elena should serve as a source of information concerning the policies of her husband and his court, and that she should as necessary influence him in the interest of her father's policies. It was no doubt to assist Elena in this function that Ivan attached to her such a large suite. But in this he miscalculated. Neither Elena nor the suite sent back any information of value. Indeed, members of this suite were apparently seduced by the Lithuanian court which was luxurious in comparison with the harsh living of the Kremlin. Ivan even began to fear that members of this suite might marry Catholic women in Lithuania, and he impressed on his daughter the need to stop such unions which would bring shame upon Muscovy. Ivan's anxieties evidently increased, for only seven months after their arrival in Vilna, he recalled the whole of her suite to Moscow, except for her confessor and two confidential secretaries.

Elena, too, must have disappointed him sadly. Although given in marriage to a man whom she had never seen, she clearly respected and even came to love him. Alexander was handsome, cultured, and able, and she was not prepared to spy on him or to try to influence him at the behest of a father who saw in her nothing more than an instrument of his policy. She did not even complain of Catholic pressure, as he had expected and even instructed her to do. She went so far as to send word to him that she felt no need for protection against Catholic persecution. Indeed, as the years passed, Elena displayed an increasing loyalty to her husband, taking his part against her father. In fact, she proved herself a woman of character, protesting against her father's aggression and calling on him to return to Lithuania the lands which he had seized. Later, when Alexander was crowned King of Poland, she was exposed to the antagonism of the Polish church and nobles who were more bigoted in their Catholicism than the Lithuanians, and she remained steadfast in her Orthodoxy. Her position was always difficult, for despite her loyalty to her husband, her religion was an embarrassment to him and, although she refused to help her father, her presence in Lithuania served his ends. In fact, she remained an instrument of his policy and, when he decided that the time was ripe, he made her the *casus belli*.

Chapter Nine

War with Sweden

THE annexation of Novgorod had been essential to the unification of Russia and a vital step in the campaign against Lithuania. But Ivan quickly found that it had also extended his responsibilities by bringing him into direct contact with his enemies. The long rivalry between Novgorod and Sweden and with the Teutonic Knights and the Hansa League, which had affected Moscow only indirectly in the past, had now become a direct concern. At the time when he wanted to concentrate his strength against Lithuania, he found that his north-western flank was exposed to attack by the Swedes and the Livonian Knights. But it was more than a matter of securing his flank. Muscovy had become a Baltic power and he was determined to secure this access to the Baltic which, like the destruction of the trade monopoly of the Hanseatic League, was necessary to the growth of Muscovite strength and nationhood.

The Swedes were the chief threat. They had long sought to bring under their control the Neva River which flowed from Lake Ladoga into the Gulf of Finland and provided the natural route between central Russia and the Baltic Sea. In 1240 Alexander Nevsky [1240–63], Prince of Novgorod, and one of Russia's national heroes, soundly defeated the Swedes on the ice of the frozen Neva, and had secured the use of this vital river for Novgorod. Rivalry between Swedes and

Novgorodtsi had continued with the Swedes invading Karelia and the Russians invading Finland. In 1323 Prince Yury of Moscow with troops from Novgorod had built the stone fortress of Oreshek [renamed Noteburg by the Swedes and Schlusselburg by Peter the Great; now called Petrokrepost]. This fortress was at the strategic point of the junction of the Neva with Lake Ladoga. Here Prince Yury had concluded with Magnus Ericsson, King of Norway and Sweden, a treaty defining the frontier which was to provide the basis of future agreements.

During the 14th century the Swedes had invaded Karelia several times. But in 1411 the Novgorodtsi had sacked Vyborg, the Swedish stronghold on the shores of the Gulf of Finland, and apart from a Swedish invasion which miscarried in 1445, Sweden and Novgorod remained at peace until the latter's annexation in 1478. In fact, during the first thirty years of Ivan III's reign, Sweden and Russia refrained from attacking each other, primarily because of internal struggles in Sweden and within Scandinavia, but also because Moscow was during this period engaged in her great venture of uniting Russia.

The people of Scandinavia had come together in the three kingdoms of Denmark, Norway, and Sweden only in the 10th century. The Swedes had then been occupied with the Finnish tribes to the north and northeast. The Norwegians had looked beyond the seas to Iceland, Scotland, and Ireland, and had given little thought to home affairs. Denmark, although the smallest of the three in area was by far the most populous and so the most powerful at the time. For some years the Baltic was, in fact, a Danish lake. But Danish power declined with the rise of Sweden, the strong rivalry of the Hanseatic League, and warfare with the neighbouring duchy of Holstein. Sweden might have become the dominant Scandinavian kingdom, but she was divided and at times reduced to anarchy by the struggles of her feudal lords to secure control of the state, or at least local independence.

Despite this internal strife and the rivalries between the ruling families, often linked by marriage, a strong movement towards the union of the three kingdoms in one Scandinavian state persisted. The union was finally achieved in the 14th century when Margaret, daughter of the Danish King, Valdemar, and wife of King Hakon of Norway, brought about the Union of Kalmar [1397]. The three kingdoms were then declared to be united forever under one king, while each retained its own laws and internal independence. But this union was to prove loose and unstable, and on the death of King Erik without heir in 1448 it came to an end.

During the period of the Scandinavian union the Swedish nobles had constantly rebelled against their Danish King and had finally driven his representatives from their country. Karl Knudson, their leader, had then become the administrator or regent of Sweden. From this time the Danish Kings were seldom able to enforce their rule over Sweden which was governed by a series of regents.

This troubled background had held the Swedes from invading Russian territory and it led Sten Sture, the then regent of Sweden, to continue the truce with Ivan. In the winter of 1475–76 Swedish ambassadors had had audience with Ivan and he had accepted their proposals to extend the peace agreement which had recently expired. In 1482 the truce was again extended for a further four years, and free navigation and movement of trade between Novgorod, Narva, and Vyborg were agreed. In 1487 Sten Sture again sent envoys to Novgorod, this time to propose extending the truce for another five years. But on this occasion Ivan refused. He had learnt of unrest along the Russo–Swedish frontier and had even had reports that an army of 60,000 Swedish troops was mobilized and ready to cross the frontier. At this time the Swedes were presumably hoping to take advantage of the fact that the Muscovite armies were engaged against Kazan. Nothing came of the Swedish invasion plans, but Ivan refused to extend the truce unless the frontier was moved westwards to the position agreed under the Treaty of Oreshek. Early in 1493, however, he had consented to the renewal of the truce, but only for eighteen months.

Meanwhile the Danes had not abandoned their great plan to revive the Scandinavian union of the three kingdoms. The Danish Kings indeed claimed Sweden and Norway as part of their realm, but their claims foundered on the opposition of the Swedes whom they were unable to subject to their rule. In 1471 King Christian, in an attempt to subdue the Swedes, suffered a severe defeat at the hands of Sten Sture. Realizing then that he could not deal alone with Sweden, he began seeking allies. His son, John, who succeeded to the Danish throne in 1481, sent his envoy to Moscow in 1493, and this was the beginning of diplomatic relations between Russia and Denmark. It resulted in a Russo-Danish alliance, concluded in Copenhagen on 9 October 1493, in which the two powers named Sweden and Lithuania as their enemies.

This alliance alarmed Sten Sture and all those who supported his policy of independence for Sweden. The fact that Ivan had openly committed himself to aiding the Danish King in his purpose of bringing Sweden back into the Scandinavian union alarmed Sten Sture all the more at this time, because opposition to his rule was growing, especially among the Swedish nobles many of whom now favoured the union under the

Danish crown. With the new stimulus of the Russo-Danish alliance, the sporadic fighting between Russians and Swedes along the Finnish frontier developed and seemed likely to become a major war.

Sten Sture learnt only two years later from secret reports by the interpreter who had taken part in the negotiations in 1493 what the terms of the Russo-Danish treaty were. This informant stated that King John of Denmark had undertaken to cede parts of Finland, including Finnish Karelia, to Ivan, if he would attack Sweden. The lands thus promised were those yielded by Yury in the treaty of 1325, which Ivan regarded as still belonging to Muscovy. He was ready to go to war to recover them, but before he could march he received a request from the Danish King, asking him to delay his offensive.

The opposition within Sweden to Sten Sture had increased until towards the end of 1494 a meeting was arranged at Kalmar to discuss with the Danes the revival of the union. King John grasped eagerly at this opportunity to gain his objective without war. But now he found his alliance with Ivan a hindrance to his attempts to win Swedish goodwill. Early in 1495 the Swedish Council of State complained to him of Ivan's plans to march on Sweden, and it was then that John sent urgently requesting Ivan to hold his hand.

The meeting at Kalmar produced no results and King John may well have sent messages once more urging his ally to march. It is highly unlikely that Ivan would have delayed his attack in any case. He had just ratified his treaty with Lithuania and he was ready to order his armies to cross the Swedish frontier. Some Russian troops were active in Finnish Karelia as early as June 1495, but it was in September that three Russian armies, one from Pskov and the others from Novgorod and Moscow, advanced against the fortress town of Vyborg. The scale of the Russian campaign reflected Ivan's determination to capture this stronghold which was the key to the Swedish defence of Finland. But after a three months' siege, the Russians had to acknowledge that their attempt to capture Vyborg was a failure, and they withdrew to Novgorod.

Ivan himself had now moved with his court to Novgorod where he was nearer to the Baltic coast and was better able to direct further operations. Without delay on the return of his armies he ordered a second expedition, directed not against Vyborg this time but farther to the north. The purpose of this expedition was apparently to lay waste parts of Finland and to strike at the morale of the Swedes who were already divided among themselves and uncertain of their ability to withstand the Russian offensive.

The Russians advanced northwards to the west of Lake Ladoga, and near to the small fortress of Nyslot they turned westwards and in February 1496 they were threatening Åbo. Here Sten Sture, disturbed by the Russian siege of Vyborg in the previous year, had assembled an army which he had transported across the Gulf of Bothnia. The morale of this army was low, especially after losses suffered in the stormy weather during this crossing from the Swedish mainland, and numerous desertions had reduced morale further. Sten Sture had nevertheless held his army at Åbo, expecting a second attempt on Vyborg. As the Russians approached Åbo from the direction of Nyslot, he led his army out to meet them. But they avoided engagement and, laying waste the land through which they marched, they returned to Novgorod with plunder and numerous prisoners. The expedition had probably achieved all that Ivan had intended. It is nonetheless difficult to understand why the Russian commanders did not engage the Swedish army at Åbo. Victory would have cut off Vyborg from all hope of support and would have enabled the Russians to starve the garrison into surrender. On the other hand Ivan's policy of avoiding risks and moving cautiously but inexorably towards his objectives without relying on dramatic victories was undoubtedly reflected in this withdrawal and it was a policy which won for him great success.

In the spring of 1496 Ivan mounted a third invasion of Swedish Finland. For this expedition he mobilized troops in the north and assembled them at the mouth of the northern Dvina River, where nearly 100 years later Archangel was to be founded. This army crossed the White Sea and, moving westwards across the Kola Peninsula, it devastated the lands along the north-eastern shores of the Gulf of Bothnia. The Russians then plunged southwards into the Savolax region of Finland, razing towns to the ground and reaching to within a few miles of Vyborg. But they made no attempt to take Vyborg, and returned to Moscow with plunder and prisoners.

Expecting further Russian invasions and unable to provide adequate defences along the extensive Russo-Swedish frontier, Sten Sture decided to take the offensive. He detached part of his army to launch a surprise attack on Russia. His objective was Ivangorod, the fortress town built in 1492 by Ivan some ten miles from the mouth of the Narova River and opposite to the great trading town of Narva on the other bank of this river. In August 1496 Swedish ships sailed up the Narova, carrying a force of 2,000 men, and took Ivangorod by surprise. The Russians offered some resistance and sent urgently to Pskov for help. Two small Russian detachments, stationed nearby, made no attempt to help and troops sent from Pskov arrived too late. The Swedes killed many of the inhabitants of Ivangorod, took others captive, and destroyed as much of the fortress as they could before withdrawing.

Ivan had planned to send another expedition into Finland, partly no doubt as a reprisal, but a dangerous revolt in Kazan made him change his plans. The destruction of Ivangorod in fact proved to be the end of the Russo–Swedish war. Ivan was now anxious to deal with the trouble in Kazan which might develop seriously. Sten Sture, alarmed by Russian devastation in Finland and fearing that Ivan would increase his pressure on Sweden, was eager for peace. In March 1497 both parties agreed in Novgorod to a truce for six years and guaranteed freedom to each other's merchants to trade.

In Sweden, however, opposition to Sten Sture had been mounting. Nobles and churchmen were openly pressing for the revival of the Scandinavian union, and the acceptance of the King of Denmark as King of Sweden and Norway. In July 1497 King John invaded Sweden and near Stockholm defeated Sten Sture's army. He was then welcomed into the capital and crowned in November.

Ivan's campaigns had greatly helped the Danish King to recover the Swedish crown. He had, in fact, amply fulfilled his part of the Russo–Danish agreement. But King John was now reluctant to cede any parts of Finland to Russia or even to discuss the matter. Ivan brought pressure to bear by threatening further invasions of Finland in 1499. John, insecure on the Swedish throne, hastened to send an envoy who arrived in Moscow in February 1500. The envoy's message contained a proposal for the marriage of Ivan's eldest son, Vasily, with John's daughter, and invited him to send his ambassadors to Sweden. Ivan acted promptly on this invitation. He chose his most able and experienced envoy, Yury Trakhaniot, to lead the embassy to Stockholm. But, although Yury left Moscow in April 1500, it was only in January of the following year that he at last succeeded in obtaining an audience with the King. He then reminded him of the Russo–Danish agreement and formally requested the cession to Moscow of Finnish Karelia. The King rejected this demand, but before further negotiations or action could be considered, Sten Sture, following upon revolts in Sweden and Norway, had displaced John and himself assumed power again.

Chapter Ten

Relations with Kazan and the Ottoman Porte

THE Tatars were an unpredictable, treacherous people. To Ivan as he planned his campaign against Lithuania, the Tatars of Kazan in particular were a constant source of uneasiness. He knew that to maintain order among them and to prevent dangerous invasions into Muscovy, he must always have an army ready to march, for they feared Russian troops. Prompt action was essential, for success by Tatar rebels in one place would bring others, rallying to share in the spoils. Rebellion would then spread through the vast Volga lands and the steppes. Kazan was the most likely powder-barrel to start such an explosion. Indeed, Muscovy was never able to relax her guard on her eastern frontier, until in 1551 Ivan III's grandson, Ivan the Terrible, conquered Kazan and suppressed the Khanate for all time.

The first reports of new unrest in Kazan reached Moscow in May 1496. The Khan, Mohammed Amin, whom Ivan had restored to power in 1487, sent word that Mamuk, Khan of the Uzbeks, who had evidently succeeded his brother, Ivak, as leader of the Siberian Khanate, was marching against Kazan. Ivan at once ordered troops from Nizhny Novgorod and Murom to proceed under the command of Prince Semeon Ryapolovsky to the Khan's defence. Mamuk withdrew on learning of the approach of the Russians. Mohammed, feeling secure again, then dismissed Ryapolovsky and his force. As they retired, the Khan's enemies sent word to Mamuk who rode swiftly to Kazan which surrendered without resistance.

Mohammed Amin had fled westward just before Mamuk's arrival and he found refuge again in Muscovy. But his flight had disturbed Ivan. Since his restoration as Khan he had been reasonably reliable, and he was an important factor in Ivan's policy of maintaining friendly relations with the Tatars. Mohammed was not only the stepson of Mengli-Girei, the Crimean Khan, but he was also linked by marriage with the two influential Nogay mirzas, Musa and Yamgurchu. Both mirzas and the Siberian Khan had continued their hostilities against the remnants of the Golden Horde, and Ivan had looked upon them as allies. Evidently he had not suspected that they were plotting rebellion. But they and other Tatars were restless for action and plunder.

In Kazan, however, the people quickly found that Mamuk, their new Khan, was a cruel master. They were regretting their betrayal of Mohammed Amin who, although given to debauchery, had at least ruled mildly. They promptly took steps to rid themselves of their new ruler. While he was away on a punitive expedition against Arsky Gorodok, a small town nearby, the people sent messages to Moscow, begging forgiveness for their betrayal and asking that Mohammed's brother, Abd al-Latif should be their new Khan. When Mamuk returned, they barred the gates of Kazan to him and, learning that Russian troops were on their way again, he fled. Shortly afterwards he died.

By April 1497 Ivan had massed two strong armies, but there was no longer any need to send them. In their place he sent a small detachment to escort Abd al-

Latif to Kazan where he was formally declared Khan. He and his people then swore loyalty to the Grand Prince of Moscow. This Tatar revolt having collapsed the Nogay and other Tatar leaders hastened to renew their protestations of friendship towards Moscow. It seemed now only a matter of providing adequately for Mohammed Amin so that Mengli-Girei, his father-in-law, would not feel affronted, and Ivan bestowed rich estates upon him in Muscovy.

In September of the following year, however, further news of Tatar unrest reached Moscow. Agalak, who had succeeded Mamuk as leader of the Siberian Khan-ate, was plotting with the Nogay Tatars and with dissident elements in Kazan to overthrow the new Khan, Abd al-Latif. Ivan was well aware of the dangers of such unrest spreading like a steppe-fire. He des-patched strong armies by land and by river to defend Kazan, and Agalak beat a hurried retreat. He made no further attempts to conquer the Khanate.

Peace and order then reigned briefly in Kazan. It was most timely for Ivan, who was at this time en-gaged against Lithuania. But in 1502 he suddenly deposed Abd al-Latif and imprisoned him in Beloozero, presumably for disobedience to the will of Moscow. Mohammed Amin was then restored to power for the fourth time. He had proved the most reliable Khan, but he, too, now betrayed Ivan. He killed several Russian merchants and even laid siege to Nizhny Nov-gorod without success. But Ivan died before he could deal with the treacherous Khan to whom he had been a benefactor.

While the Tatars were an immediate threat to be dealt with promptly, the Ottoman Porte loomed as a massive potential danger. Ivan did not underestimate the might of the Sultan or deceive himself in thinking that he could withstand a determined Turkish advance northwards across the steppelands and into Muscovy. Fortunately for his plans, Bayazit II was engaged in other directions, especially in south-eastern Europe and in the Mediterranean. Ivan feared, nevertheless, that the Sultan might reach some agreement with Poland and Lithuania or that he might restrain his vassal, Mengli-Girei, from carrying out his part of the alliance with Muscovy. These were dangers more likely than the great danger that the Sultan would summon the Tatars as fellow Moslems to join the Turks in the conquest of Muscovy.

To secure himself in the south Ivan with his usual caution sought an alliance with the Sultan or at least an understanding which would set his mind at rest as to Turkish intentions. He had at this time almost certainly exchanged ambassadors with Sultan Mohammed II and merchants had traded between Moscow and Constantinople. After Mohammed's death in 1482, however, diplomatic exchanges had apparently lapsed and trade had fallen off sharply. He had tried several times through Mengli-Girei to revive relations with the Porte, but without result.

In the 1490s further deterioration of trade caused Ivan to take firm action. Russian merchants had been complaining strongly of high-handed action by Turkish officials in Azov and Kaffa, the two chief points for the entry of Russian merchandise. Early in 1492 Ivan imposed a ban on all Russian trade with the Porte. It was a drastic action, which angered the Turks who in both towns suffered serious loss of revenue as a result. But the ban also caused losses to the Russian merchants. A few months later Ivan, anxious to revive and increase this trade and at the same time to avoid offending the Turks, sent a letter to the Sultan, setting out the Russian complaints, which had led to this embargo and proposing negotiations.

This letter, sent to the Crimean Khan to be forwarded to the Sultan, drew no reply for nearly three years. As the months passed Ivan became increasingly disturbed. His envoys to Mengli-Girei regularly asked the reasons for the the Sultan's silence, and received neither reply nor explanations. During these years, however, Bayazit was completely absorbed in southeastern Europe, where his military operations were on a massive scale. He was also greatly concerned over the danger that the Christian powers might unite to launch a crusade against him. His brother and rival, Jem, had fled to the west in 1482 and, supported as he was by the Pope, might possibly have been used to spearhead such a movement against the Ottoman Porte. Ivan must have known something about these preoccupations of the Sultan at this time, and it is surprising that he should have expected a reply on a comparatively minor matter of trade with Russia.

By the spring of 1495, however, peace had returned to south-eastern Europe and Bayazit's brother, Jem, had died. The Sultan was now free to attend to the matters which he had neglected, including the complaints from Moscow. In 1495 he appointed as governor of Kaffa his son, Mohammed, who took prompt action to remove the restraints on Russian merchants. He also sent an envoy to Ivan to assure him that he would have no further grounds for complaints. The Turkish envoy travelled no farther than Kiev, however, when Lithuanian officials arrested him. Two members of his party subsequently reached Moscow. Ivan, at this time in Novgorod directing his campaign against Sweden, was furious to learn of this Lithuanian interference. He sent angry complaints to Vilna and demanded that the Turkish envoy should be allowed to proceed freely to Moscow. Alexander was determined, however, to do nothing to assist in the alliance of his two greatest enemies, Moscow and the Ottoman Porte, and he merely replied that he had sent the Turk back to Kaffa.

Convinced that this envoy had come not merely from the governor of Kaffa, but also from the Sultan himself, Ivan without delay appointed Mikhail A. Pleshcheev to lead an embassy to Constantinople, for he was eager to establish diplomatic relations with the Porte not only to secure himself as far as possible against Turkish interference, while he was engaged against Lithuania, but also to facilitate trade and for reasons of national prestige.

In Kaffa, Pleshcheev conveyed to Mohammed the list of grievances of the Russian merchants. He then proceeded to Constantinople where he was received in audience by the Sultan, the first accredited Russian ambassador to be so received. Bayazit treated him with every courtesy, promising facilities for trade, and he welcomed the proposal for the regular exchange of ambassadors. Pleshcheev returned to Moscow in February 1498 and reported glowingly on the success of his mission which was to be followed by the despatch of the Sultan's ambassadors to the Grand Prince. But no ambassadors came and a year later, in the spring of 1499, Ivan sent another mission, this time headed by Alexander Golokhvastov, to Kaffa and Constantinople.

Ivan had already raised his embargo on trade and Russian merchants had set out for Kaffa. Golokhvastov's instructions were to state that, relying on the Sultan's promises, Ivan had allowed his merchants to return to the Turkish markets. He was also to urge the Sultan to send his ambassadors without further delay and to encourage his merchants to travel with their wares into Russia. Bayazit again sent messages of goodwill to Ivan, but he gave no indication that he would send his envoys. To Ivan it now became obvious that he could not hope for any political agreement with the Sultan. A further disappointment was that, despite the Sultan's assurances, Russian merchants suffered as before at the hands of Turkish officials.

Ivan sent no further mission to Constantinople. Trade continued and he made his complaints to the governor of Kaffa as before. The Sultan himself sent envoys to Moscow in the autumn of 1500, but they were halted in Kaffa by the refusal of the Crimean Khan to provide escorts for their onward journey across the dangerous no-man's-land of the steppes. Indeed, Mengli-Girei may well have been active earlier in hindering the exchange of embassies between Moscow and Constantinople and the formation of an alliance between the Sultan and the Grand Prince. He was already the vassal of the Sultan, but probably enjoyed considerable autonomy, especially while Bayazit was occupied in south-eastern Europe and the Mediterranean. Moreover, he was allied with Ivan, but his Khanate lay between the Ottoman Porte and Muscovy and direct alliance of these two powers would surely result in some further constriction of his freedom. Nevertheless the chief reason for the failure of the Sultan to respond to Ivan's advances was probably the fact that alliance with Muscovy offered him no real advantage. Also Ivan's agreement and dynastic alliance with Alexander in 1494 may well have aroused doubts in Bayazit's mind as to his reliability as an ally against Lithuania and Poland. But, while Ivan was undoubtedly disappointed in his attempts to form an alliance with the Sultan, he had the consolation of close alliance with the Crimean Khan and, at that time, with Stephen of Moldavia.

The agreement, directed against Lithuania–Poland, made between Mengli-Girei and Stephen, also suited Ivan's plans admirably. But they were both difficult and unpredictable allies on whom he had to keep a close watch. Mengli-Girei was over-greedy and ambitious and soon his plans for attacking Lithuania were disturbing Ivan. Early in the 1490s the Khan had decided to facilitate his invasions of southern Lithuania by moving his headquarters from Perekop to a new stronghold, called Tyaginka, which he had erected on the right bank of the Dnieper. Already, too, he was planning a new advance base which was to be Kiev itself. Ivan's misgivings increased. He mistrusted the Crimean Tatars and did not welcome any permanent extension of their frontiers north of the Dnieper any more than he welcomed the prospect of his two routes to the Black Sea, by way of the Dnieper and Bug Rivers, being controlled by the Khan. The other and even more important reason for Ivan's strong objection to Mengli-Girei's new base was that he himself considered Kiev and the Dnieper lands to be part of his patrimony. He planned to recover them as soon as possible, and he foresaw clashes with the Tatars in Tyaginka, and war if they occupied Kiev. He made strong representations to Mengli-Girei, urging him to concentrate on attacking Lithuania, not on building new strongholds on the Dnieper. In fact, the Crimean Tatars were very active at this time in invading Lithuania, and Ivan could have no complaint on this score. He was probably pleased, however, when in the autumn of 1493 Alexander in a rare counter-attack sent troops south who destroyed Tyaginka and when in retaliation Mengli-Girei himself led a large force which devastated vast regions of Podolia.

The next three years witness a lull in Tatar aggression against Lithuania. Mengli-Girei was probably preoccupied with rebuilding Tyaginka and erecting the fortress of Ochakov on the shores of the Black Sea. Ivan in this period had the delicate task of explaining to his ally the peace treaty which he had made with Alexander and the marriage of his daughter to him. His problem was not only to explain his own apparent change in policy, but also to hold the Khan as his ally, ready at the right time to resume the offensive against Lithuania. For nearly a year Ivan delayed informing the Khan and when he did the Khan expressed his disappointment, especially over the delay in letting him know of the treaty. Ivan then made some efforts to effect a temporary reconciliation between Mengli-Girei and Alexander, designed to keep the former as his ally while not breaking his new agreement with the latter. His efforts were, however, overtaken in 1497 by a Polish campaign against the Turks and Tatars which ended in disaster.

Jan Olbracht, the King of Poland, mobilized an army of 80,000 troops for this crusade. His brother, Vladislav of Hungary, had signed a six-year truce with the Sultan and so could not participate openly. Alexander informed Ivan that he would aid his brother in the Polish campaign. The complication was that Moldavia, whose ruler, Stephen, had committed many acts of aggression against Poland, stood in the way of the Polish advance against Turkey, and was also allied with the Crimean Khan. Ivan at once realized the seriousness of the situation. In August 1497, when he believed that both Poles and Lithuanians were attacking Moldavia and might well have conquered his ally, he despatched two envoys to Alexander. They conveyed Ivan's strong warning that Moldavia was Moscow's ally and that Stephen was bound to him not only by alliance but also by marriage. Furthermore Alexander was reminded that in his treaty with Ivan he had undertaken to treat the latter's friends and enemies as his friends and enemies. Bluntly Ivan ordered him to remain at peace with Stephen. Alexander now found himself in a most difficult position. He wanted to support his brother, Jan Olbracht, but the dangers of doing so were forbidding. The Crimean Khan would attack him in the south and Ivan, treating their agreement of 1494 as a dead letter, would attack from the east. He tried to compromise by detaching part of his forces to serve with the Polish armies and by withdrawing his remaining troops to Vilna.

In August the Poles invaded Moldavia, intending to capture the capital, Suceava, before marching into the Turkish lands along the Black Sea coast. Stephen resisted. His capital repelled the Polish attempts to take it and then Stephen himself with his small army inflicted a crushing defeat on the Poles at Bukovina in October [1497].

At this time Alexander, judging that the Crimean Khan would be tied down waiting to defend his lands against the Poles sweeping through Moldavia, launched an attack on the rebuilt Tatar stronghold on the Dnieper. This time his attempt to take Tyaginka failed completely.

Poland and Lithuania paid dearly for their attacks on Moldavia and the Crimean Khanate. Stephen and Mengli-Girei had appealed to the Sultan to punish both countries and in May 1498 a great Turkish army, 40,000 to 60,000 strong, advanced across the Danube and Dniester Rivers into Poland. The Turks destroyed all before them and pressed northwards as far as Warsaw before they retired, taking 10,000 prisoners with them to sell into slavery. In November the Turks again invaded Poland, this time laying waste the southern regions.

The first Turkish invasion of Poland alarmed Alexander. His fear was that Mengli-Girei, supported by Stephen and by the Sultan, would launch a similar attack on Lithuania. He decided therefore to appeal to Ivan to intercede with both rulers and to persuade them to make peace with him. Ivan undertook this mediation on behalf of his son-in-law. But Prince Semeon Romodanovsky, sent to the Crimea for this purpose, also had his secret instructions, which were to assure Mengli-Girei of Ivan's support no matter what his intentions might be against Lithuania; it was, in fact, a clear encouragement to him to continue his aggression.

Thus towards the close of the 15th century, Ivan found himself in a strong position to go to war against Lithuania. Kazan and the Nogay Tatars were in one of their periods of calm and no outbreaks among them seemed likely. Mengli-Girei was his firm ally and at all times eager to attack Lithuania and Poland. Stephen of Moldavia was also his ally, but in his manoeuvring to prevent his small country being swallowed up by strong neighbours he was not dependable. The Sultan, although bound by no alliance with Moscow, was evidently prepared to encourage Mengli-Girei, Stephen, and others to attack Poland and Lithuania. In the north, Denmark was Moscow's ally and Sweden was most unlikely to go to the aid of Lithuania. Alexander, who knew he could not stand alone against the might of Muscovy, could count on no outside support and, indeed, his position seemed to grow weaker as Ivan's grew stronger.

Chapter Eleven

War with Lithuania 1500—03

BY the spring of 1500 Ivan was ready to march on Lithuania. The sole obstacle in his way was the Russo–Lithuanian treaty of peace, made only six years earlier and sealed by the marriage of his daughter with Alexander. But this was not a real obstacle. Indeed, Ivan may well have agreed to this marriage, intending to use his daughter as a pretext for war when the time was ripe. His attitude, that any perfidy was permissible so long as it advanced the national interest, may have been morally unjustifiable, but it was certainly productive of results.

At this very time one of the most prominent officials in Florence was Nicolo Machiavelli, who subsequently distilled his experience of rulers and their methods in his treatise *The Prince*. In one chapter "Concerning the way in which princes keep faith", he wrote: "Everyone admits how praiseworthy it is in a prince to keep faith and to live with integrity and not with craft. Nevertheless our experience has been that those princes who have done great things have held good faith of little account and have known how to circumvent the intellect of men by craft, and in the end have overcome those who have relied on their word". Machiavelli had in mind, as he wrote, the rulers of Italy, France and ancient Rome, but he might equally have been writing of his contemporary, Ivan the Great.

In the spring of 1499 Ivan had seized on a report

from Vilna, which seemed to offer grounds for declaring war. The report was from a Muscovite official in Lithuania, named Feodor Shestakov, who had contact with Elena, Alexander's wife. It stated that strong pressure was being exerted on her and on all Orthodox believers in Lithuania to accept the Uniate church. The Uniate bishop of Smolensk and Metropolitan-designate of Kiev, Iosif Bolgarinovich, and the influential secretary to Alexander, Ivan Sapieha, who also held some appointment at the court of Elena, were said to be the leaders of this religious drive.

Ivan at once sent Boyar Ivan Mamonov to Vilna to obtain confirmation from Elena of the alleged persecution. But she was unable to receive him because of illness. On two further occasions envoys set out from Moscow only to return without having seen her. Elena may have been ill or have declined to receive her father's envoys at her husband's request or of her own free will. She was always to show herself unwilling to serve as the instrument of her father's policy against Alexander and her adopted homeland.

Evidence of the persecution of the Orthodox in Lithuania came from another quarter early in 1500. Prince Semeon Belsky sent word to Moscow that he was eager to swear allegiance to Ivan. His brother, Prince Feodor, had gone over to Moscow many years earlier, and he now gave as the reason for his belated change of heart the religious persecution in Lithuania. He, too, named Iosif Bolgarinovich as the leader of this religious campaign, and added that monks of the Bernadine Order were actively helping him in this persecution.

Semeon Belsky's transfer of allegiance to Moscow in April 1500 was the beginning of a wave of defections. The Princes of Mosalsk and of Khotetovo and many among the most prominent of Alexander's subjects in the Serpeisk and Mtsensk regions acknowledged the sovereignty of Ivan. Then, shortly afterwards, Princes Vasily Shemyachich and Semeon Mozhaisky, direct descendants of the chief enemies of Ivan III's father, Vasily II, declared themselves the subjects of Moscow. Alexander had granted them extensive lands, which were thus transferred or ready to be annexed by Muscovy. All gave as the reason for their tardy change of allegiance the persecution of the Orthodox in Lithuania.

In accepting these princes as his subjects, Ivan was breaking his agreement with Alexander. The treaty of 1494 had established the frontier between the two countries and had specified that they should not accept defectors from each other's territories. Ivan nevertheless showed no hesitation in accepting these new subjects, and he loudly proclaimed their complaints of religious persecution as his justification. Indeed, he was preparing to make this the ground for declaring war against Lithuania, rather than his involved and legally tenuous claims to the Lithuanian lands, occupied by Orthodox Russians.

The degree of pressure brought to bear on Elena and the extent of the persecution suffered by the Orthodox in Lithuania at this time are matters of conjecture. It was true that Alexander had not built his wife an Orthodox chapel or maintained an Orthodox suite to attend on her as he had promised, but it may be doubted whether he pressed her unreasonably to become a convert to Roman Catholicism or allowed others to do so. Similarly it is doubtful whether any wide-scale campaign of persecution was mounted against the Orthodox in Lithuania at this time. In fact, Alexander, aware of the wavering loyalty of his predominantly Orthodox subjects in his western and south-western principalities, would hardly have encouraged such a religious movement. Nevertheless numerous incidents involving the Orthodox undoubtedly took place, for neither the Roman Catholics nor the Orthodox were remarkable for their tolerance or charity. This would not, however, have been enough to cause the princes, surrounded by their *druzhini* or private armies and wielding great power in their principalities, to defect. The most probable explanation is that they swore allegiance to Ivan primarily because they realized that in the impending war he was more likely to emerge victorious, and that by anticipating this outcome they would save their estates and their own skins.

As the threat of war became more ominous, Alexander anxiously sought to placate his father-in-law or at least to delay hostilities. In 1499 he sent an embassy to Moscow to announce the treaty that he had made with Stephen of Moldavia and to propose an alliance against the Sultan as well as some understanding with Ivan which would, he hoped, ward off the danger of war with Muscovy. His envoy also made a concession concerning Ivan's title, a matter which had constantly bedevilled relations with Muscovy. Alexander had in the 1494 treaty acknowledged Ivan's title as being "by the grace of God, Sovereign of all Russia", but despite Ivan's repeated protests he had consistently referred to him on all occasions merely as "Grand Prince of Moscow". Alexander now undertook to use the full title in future on the condition that Ivan signed an undertaking to recognize Kiev as part of Lithuania. It was a foolish proposition which was wholly unacceptable and served only to anger Ivan.

In the spring of 1500 Alexander sent his last embassy to Moscow. This time the ambassador, Stanislav Kishka, without conditions of any kind addressed Ivan by his full title. He then conveyed Alexander's strong denials of Ivan's numerous complaints of religious persecution and made the counter-charge that by accepting Lithuanian defectors in Muscovy Ivan had broken the terms of the 1494 treaty. Finally, Kishka expressed his master's desire to meet the wishes of his father-in-law and to negotiate a peace with the Crimean Khan with Ivan's mediation. A few months earlier Ivan had sent Mamonov as his envoy to Vilna with a note on the terms on which Mengli-Girei was prepared to agree a peace with Lithuania, and it was on the basis of these demands, which were exorbitant, that Alexander was ready to negotiate.

Ivan merely interpreted this conciliatory approach as further evidence of Lithuanian demoralization and weakness. In his reply he repeated in full detail all the charges concerning religious persecution of his daughter, Elena, and of the Orthodox in Lithuania, and he now spoke in more threatening tones. His confidence in the strength of his position had been boosted further about this time by the defection of Belsky and the other princes, and he felt no need to delay operations. Within a few days of the departure of Kishka to report to Alexander, a courier set out for Vilna with the formal Muscovite declaration of war.

On 3 May 1500 the first of the three Russian armies marched from Moscow. Commanded by Yakov Zakharin, it advanced into the Seversk region. The town of Bryansk on the Desna River was captured, apparently without offering resistance. The army then occupied the extensive lands, comprising the principalities of Princes Shemyachich and Mozhaisky, who had defected earlier. The whole of the lower Desna region was quickly annexed and the people swore allegiance to Moscow.

At this time the second army, commanded by Yury Zakharin, was advancing towards the fortified town of

Dorogobuzh on the Dnieper River, forty-five miles to the east of Smolensk. The Russians captured Dorogobuzh, again meeting no resistance. It was an important gain, for this fortress would serve as a base from which to attack Smolensk, the key to Ivan's strategy for recovering and holding the northern Russian lands in Lithuanian possession.

The third army was stationed in the north. It was to stand in reserve while the other two armies were advancing on their objectives. Its task was then to take Toropets and the whole region which lay exposed to invasion from the principality of Vyazma, gained by Ivan under the treaty of 1494.

Alexander was inactive, as though paralyzed, during these opening stages of the Russian campaign. He probably realized that he could do nothing to defend the lower Desna region where the local princes with their armed retinues had already gone over to Moscow. But the capture of Dorogobuzh stirred him to action. He saw that Smolensk was now threatened and he attached the same importance to retaining this stronghold as Ivan attached to taking it. He therefore concentrated his forces under the command of Prince Konstantin Ostrozhsky to defend it.

Learning of the presence of the main Lithuanian army near Smolensk, Ivan hurriedly moved up reinforcements, and re-formed the army under the supreme command of Prince Daniil Shchenya. On 14 July 1500 on the banks of the Vedrosha River, to the west of Dorogobuzh, the Russian and Lithuanian armies joined in battle. The fighting was savage and the casualties heavy on both sides, but the Russians emerged as decisive victors. The Lithuanian army was destroyed and all who did not perish on the field were taken prisoner, including Ostrozhsky and most of his senior commanders. Russian casualties were also heavy

and Shchenya sent urgently to Ivan requesting reinforcements. The way was now clear for him to march
on Smolensk, but Ivan was always cautious and, even
when the reinforcements had arrived, Shchenya presumably on his orders did not march westwards, but
rested his troops near the scene of victory.

Meanwhile the other two Russian armies had advanced farther into Lithuania. In the north the
governor of Novgorod, Andrei Chelyadin, commanded
the army which took the stronghold of Toropets. This
brought into Ivan's possession the region which swept
upwards behind the Velikie Luki enclave. In the south
Yakov Zakharin took the town of Putivl on the Seym
River, thus strengthening the Russian positions there
in readiness for a new campaign to take Kiev.

The operations of these four months of the summer
of 1500 had thus brought Ivan tremendous gains,
representing more than half of the objectives which he
had set out to achieve. He now held the whole of the
basin of the Oka River, much of the territory in the
basins of the Desna and Seym Rivers. In the north the
capture of the Toropets region and the principality of
Vyazma had given him possession of the upper reaches
of the Dnieper and West Dvina Rivers. Moreover, his
army had inflicted such a defeat on the Lithuanians at
the Vedrosha River, that they were completely de-
moralized, and he could look forward to achieving all
his objectives in the near future.

During these same months Lithuania had also suffered severely from Tatar invasions. In the spring of
1500 Mengli-Girei had sent a strong force under the
command of his sons to ravage the southern parts of
Lithuania and Poland. The Tatars had laid waste
Volhynia and razed to the ground the important town
of Lutsk on the Styr River. The main Tatar army had
advanced north and west to the Vistula, plundering

the towns and devastating the land. They returned to Perekop in July, laden with booty and prisoners. A few weeks later the Khan launched an even larger force into Lithuania and Poland. This time the Tatars crossed the Vistula and ravaged a greater area before returning with, it was claimed, 50,000 prisoners.

The Tatar operations were carried out independently of Ivan's summer campaign. The two rulers had agreed to coordinate their attacks on Lithuania and to keep each other fully informed. For some reason, however, Ivan deliberately delayed for more than three months before sending word to the Khan that he had declared war on Alexander. Mengli-Girei knew, of course, of the Muscovite campaign and of its successes and in August he wrote to congratulate his ally and to suggest a joint attack on Kiev. Early in the winter Ivan sent the reply that his forces would move against Smolensk in the spring of 1501, and he proposed that the Tatars should invade the enemy's territory, advancing northwards across the Pripyat River against Pinsk, Slutsk, and Minsk. But these attempts at the coordination of their operations proved a failure.

Meanwhile Alexander was desperately seeking allies. He had tried to negotiate with the Crimean Khan, but he had relied on Russian mediation, and Ivan had taken care to prevent understanding between them. In fact, he had instructed Prince Ivan Kubensky, his envoy to the Crimea in the spring of 1500, to impress on the Khan that he was counting on the Tatars to join him in a strong offensive against Lithuania. The two large-scale Tatar attacks had followed.

Realizing belatedly that Ivan was making every effort to confound his relations with the Crimean Khan, Alexander sent word direct to Mengli-Girei of his readiness to negotiate a formal treaty. Seeing the possibility of reviving payment of regular tribute and other concessions, the Khan sent safe-conducts for a Lithuanian ambassador. Alexander chose for this task Prince Dmitri Putyatich, the *voevoda* of Kiev, and his instructions made it clear that his main task was to undermine the Khan's confidence in Ivan. He was to warn him that, if Ivan were to annex parts of the Ukraine, he would have a treacherous neighbour who would bring only trouble to the Tatars. Putyatich was also to offer the Khan annual tribute, levied from certain Lithuanian districts in the south. Unfortunately no record of this mission has survived. Clearly, however, Putyatich, if received in audience by the Khan, was unable to impress him or shake his confidence in his ally, for Tatar attacks on Lithuania continued unabated.

Alexander himself apparently expected few results from this mission to the Khan, for at the same time he sent an envoy to the Khan's most hated enemy, the Golden Horde, which lingered on, a shadow of its former greatness. He proposed to Shaikh Ahmad, its Khan, a joint treaty with him and with the Nogay Tatars. The plan which his envoy outlined was that Lithuania, Hungary, and Poland would join to attack Muscovy from the west, while the Nogay Tatars and the Golden Horde would attack from the south and east. The chief interest of Shaikh Ahmad was to secure Lithuanian support for a campaign against the Crimean Khanate, but Alexander's envoy argued strongly that it would be best to wait until Muscovy had been subdued, for then the Crimean Tatars could be handled with ease. It was an unrealistic plan which showed that Alexander was clutching at every possible chance of help. Nevertheless, while unable to make any impression of Muscovy, Shaikh Ahmad, merely by the existence of his Horde, distracted Mengli-Girei from repeating the terrible invasions of Lithuania which he had carried out in 1500.

Alexander's other attempts to find allies gave rise only to diplomatic interventions on his behalf, which produced no results. Stephen of Moldavia became his most active ally in urging Ivan to make peace, but Stephen refused to be drawn into war against Muscovy. Despite his personal antagonism towards the Jagiellons who ruled in Hungary, Lithuania, and Poland, Stephen was most afraid of the Sultan who might well seek to annex Moldavia. Ivan had in 1497 counselled Alexander and Stephen to make peace, because it had then suited his policy. Two years later they had formed an alliance, directed against Turkey in which they were probably joined by the rulers of Poland and Hungary, and Stephen was to prove a more ardent ally to Alexander than to Ivan. In 1500 he sent his envoy to Moscow to urge Ivan not to go to war against Alexander and he continued to make strenuous efforts to bring about peace between Moscow and Vilna. Moreover, in June 1500 he sent an ambassador to the Crimean Khan to persuade him not to march against Lithuania. But his attempts to mediate were in vain, for both Ivan and Mengli-Girei were determined to pursue their campaigns.

Early in 1501 Alexander's brothers, Vladislav of Hungary and Jan Olbracht of Poland, sent ambassadors to Moscow to plead for peace. They even voiced vague threats of military intervention and reprisals. But Ivan was not impressed and curtly rejected their proposals. He expressed himself ready to negotiate a peace, but on terms that he would dictate when the Lithuanian ambassadors had arrived in Moscow. He nevertheless ordered a cessation of hostilities along the frontier, pending their arrival. But at the same time he sent word to Mengli-Girei that Alexander's offers of peace had proved unacceptable and that he was opening a new campaign without delay. The Lithuanian ambassadors did not, in fact, come. Jan Olbracht died in June and Alexander then became King of Poland as well as being Grand Prince of Lithuania. As ruler of both countries he may have felt more confident of his ability to meet Muscovite aggression, but, if so, his new confidence was misplaced.

Ivan's campaign in the summer of 1501 again involved attacks on Lithuania from three directions. Princes Shemyachich and Mozhaisky were ordered to advance in the south and Ivan urged the Crimean Khan to invade Lithuania, proceeding up the southern Bug River into Podolia and Volhynia.

Ivan concentrated his main armies in the north, directing his campaign against Smolensk. The strongest of the three Muscovite forces was stationed in the principality of Tver. He had appointed in command of this army his son, Vasily, who was, however, supported by the most outstanding and experienced of the Russian commanders, namely Princes Daniil Shchenya, Vladimir Mikulinsky, and D. A. Shein. This army was, however, held in reserve in Tver, while in April 1501 a smaller army moved westwards from Moscow and another stronger force moved southwards from Novgorod. But for reasons not all of which are known, the extensive plans for this summer campaign were cancelled.

In the autumn of 1501, however, major operations resulted in a further decisive victory for Ivan. Strong reinforcements were sent in September to Starodub, the headquarters of Shemyachich and Mozhaisky, who then advanced northwards towards Smolensk. Near Mstislavl, some fifty miles to the south of Smolensk, the Lithuanian army engaged them on 4 November. The fighting was long and severe, but the Muscovite force ended by completely crushing the Lithuanians, killing 7,000 and taking many prisoners. Surprisingly Shemyachich and Mozhaisky made no attempt to take Mstislavl which was at their mercy, and they did not continue their advance to Smolensk. Evidently their task was to destroy the Lithuanian army and then withdraw.

At this time Ivan's troops were also active on his north-western frontier against the Livonian Knights. The Master of the Livonian Order, Von Plettenberg, an able and energetic leader, had early in 1501 formed an alliance with Alexander against Ivan. The first aggression under this alliance was an attempt by the garrison of Narva to capture Ivangorod, but this failed. The Livonian Knights then prepared to launch an attack on Pskov. Ivan ordered to Pskov the army which had set out from Moscow in April to invade Lithuania. But for some weeks this army merely stood by while the Livonians attacked the lands along the Pskov frontier. Only after the Pskovtsi had sent bitter complaints to Ivan, did he order this army to march. The Muscovite and Pskov troops engaged Von Plettenberg's army on 27 August on the banks of the Seritsa River, and the Livonians, using their artillery to full advantage, put the Russians to flight. They then laid siege to Izborsk, some seven miles to the south. The town resisted stoutly, but the Livonians took and burnt to the ground Ostrov, a town on the Velikaya River. In September, having laid waste large areas of the Republic of Pskov, Von Plettenberg withdrew his troops into Livonia.

Ivan took immediate action to deal with the Livonians. Joined with the Lithuanian army they could have amounted to a serious threat to his plans. He appointed his most distinguished commander, Prince Daniil Shchenya, to lead a strong force, comprising troops from Moscow, Novgorod, Tver, and Pskov, supported by a numerous Tatar detachment, against the Livonians. Setting out in November 1501, Shchenya's army came up with the main German force at Helmed, not far from Dorpat. Again the fighting was fierce and the Germans made full use of their artillery, but they could not stand against the Russian army and suffered a crushing defeat. The Russians then surged through the northern parts of Livonia, laying waste all in their path. It is said that 40,000 Livonians were killed or taken captive. Von Plettenberg, his army almost annihilated at Helmed and his country devastated, was no longer a danger to Muscovy.

In the summer of 1501 Ivan was also troubled by the Golden Horde. Alexander, following the policy of his father, Casimir, had towards the end of the previous year sent envoys to the Horde to conclude an alliance against Moscow. The plan which was apparently agreed was that the Tatars of the Golden Horde would invade Ryazan, Murom, and other southern principalities of Muscovy, while the Nogay Tatars invaded Kazan.

The Golden Horde moved from Saray, its main headquarters on the Volga River, early in 1501. Two sons of Ahmad, Shaikh Ahmad and Seyyid Ahmad, led the two Tatar forces which combined at a point near the junction of the Don and the Medveditsa Rivers. They then proceeded up the Don to its junction with the Tikhaya Sosna where in July they established a stronghold.

This western movement of the Golden Horde alarmed Ivan and, even more, Mengli-Girei who was convinced that Ahmad's sons were advancing against his Khanate. He had just despatched a large-scale expedition into Lithuania when he learnt that the

Tatars of the Golden Horde had reached the Don. He at once turned eastwards to meet his great enemy. By the time he had reached the Donets River, however, he realized that Shaikh Ahmad, who after a quarrel with his brother was in sole command, was marching against Muscovy and not against the Crimea. Mengli-Girei nevertheless continued his advanced as far as the Tikhaya Sosna River, where he erected a fortress opposite the position of the Golden Horde troops. Then, confident that Shaikh Ahmad intended no harm to his Khanate, Mengli-Girei withdrew his army. His attitude was plainly that, since the Horde as an ally of Alexander was marching against Muscovy, it was for Ivan to do the fighting. Evidently even he realized, however, that such behaviour towards an ally was contemptible, for he made numerous excuses for the withdrawal of his Tatars.

Ivan had already in response to an earlier message from Mengli-Girei sent troops and had then ordered a strong army to proceed down the Don to Tikhaya Sosna. There the Russians found both fortresses unmanned. While Mengli-Girei had withdrawn to the Crimea, Shaikh Ahmad had advanced westward towards Rylsk on the Seym River. Ivan immediately sent orders to Princes Shemyachich and Mozhaisky to march from Starodub to deal with these Tatars. At the same time he sent envoys to Mengli-Girei angrily insisting that the Khan should march against this old enemy who was now disrupting their joint campaign against Lithuania. Mengli-Girei did not reply. Meanwhile Shemyachich and Mozhaisky were driving Shaikh Ahmad's Tatars from the region of the Seym River, and they retired into quarters on the banks of the Donets River for the winter.

Shaikh Ahmad was now in a desperate position. His Tatars were defeated in spirit and many had deserted, some of them to the Crimean Horde. Food, fodder, and horses were lacking for any further advance. Strong enemies waited to attack from the north and south-west, and he could not count on help from Lithuania or from the Nogay Tatars. Finally in December [1502] he made proposals to Ivan for peace. Some agreement was negotiated by which Shaikh Ahmad probably undertook to refrain from attacking Muscovy, while Ivan promised to give no assistance to the Crimean Khan against him. At this time, too, the Nogay Tatar leaders, Musa and Yamgurchu, made their peace with Moscow. Ivan was thus secure for a time from threats of attacks by Alexander's allies in the east and south.

In fact, the Golden Horde was nearing its final demise. Even without Muscovite help Mengli-Girei was more than strong enough to deal with this most hated of his enemies. Early in June [1502] his warriors annihilated the army of Shaikh Ahmad who with a few companions managed to escape. Thus the Golden Horde which from Sarai had dominated the Russian lands for more than two centuries had passed almost completely from the scene.

In 1502, the third year of the Russo-Lithuanian war, Ivan again planned his campaign on a grand scale. His goal was the capture of Smolensk, the stronghold dominating the extensive west Russian territories which he was determined to recover. His main army was under the command of his son, Dmitri, then only 21 years of age, but many of the most experienced Russian commanders again served under him and exercised the real command. This army set out from Moscow on 14 July and, advancing rapidly westwards, laid siege to Smolensk. Ivan was so sure of the success of this operation that he told his son that reinforcements would only be sent if Alexander himself marched to relieve the fortress-city.

In the north around Novgorod and Pskov, Ivan had posted another strong army in full campaign readiness under the command of Prince Daniil Shchenya. The purpose of this army was to engage any Lithuanian forces that might be sent to help the besieged garrison in Smolensk. But also this army was standing ready to meet any attacks by the Master of the Livonian Order, Von Plettenberg. He had suffered a severe defeat at Helmed when his army had been virtually destroyed, but the Russians had not forgotten his victory on the banks of the Seritsa River, and they did not underestimate his ability to mobilize a new army.

For his main support in this campaign to take Smolensk, however, Ivan was counting on Mengli-Girei. As Dmitri marched his army from Moscow, Ivan began rushing messages to the Crimea, urging the Khan to launch a major attack on Lithuania without delay. The Tatar army should, he proposed, follow the route used before, northwards to Kiev and on to Turov, Slutsk, and Minsk, but then, turning northeast, the Tatars would join up with the main Russian army before Smolensk. Mengli-Girei had, in fact, already sent his army, under the command of his youngest sons, Feti-Girei and Burnash-Girei, three days before Ivan's courier arrived. Said to number 90,000 warriors, this was one of the largest expeditions that the Khan had yet launched. He acted at once on Ivan's proposals and sent new orders to his sons to press northwards even to Vilna and also to make contact with Dmitri's army at Smolensk.

Ivan's careful strategy now seemed assured of success. Lithuania could not hope to stand against such a massing of armies, attacking from different directions and Smolensk was bound to fall. In the event, however,

Ivan's plans miscarried. The garrison and people of Smolensk defended their stronghold with great spirit. The Russians made repeated assaults against its walls and gates without success. They captured Orsha on the Dnieper River, some sixty miles to the west. They ravaged the land as far north as Polotsk and as far south as the Berezina River. But they could not take Smolensk and after a siege of three months Dmitri withdrew his army and returned to Moscow.

In the north Shchenya was unable to render any help to the siege force, for he was engaged against the Livonians. Von Plettenberg in the spring of 1502 made two raids, one on Ivangorod and the other on Krasny, a small town in the extreme south of the Republic of Pskov. Shchenya, thus alerted, awaited the main Livonian attack, but it did not come for several months. The Livonian army crossed the frontier south of Lake Chudskoe, made for Izborsk, and then on 6 September laid siege to Pskov itself. The Pskovtsi managed to defend their city and Von Plettenberg, learning that a Russian army was advancing rapidly from Novgorod, retreated southwards.

Shchenya's army, which was more or less the same as that which had defeated the Livonians in the previous year, pursued Von Plettenberg and engaged his force at Lake Smolino, some forty miles due south of Pskov. This time the Russians were not the victors. Some accounts of the battle claimed a resounding success for the Livonians, but it was an indecisive battle in which both sides suffered heavy losses and neither was eager to re-engage. Von Plettenberg retreated into Livonia. Shchenya returned to Novgorod. But the Livonians had throughout most of the year succeeded in holding Shchenya's large army in the north. Only in December could it advance into Lithuania and by that time Dmitri had already raised the siege of Smolensk and withdrawn his army.

Ivan's greatest disappointment, however, was the failure of the Khan's two sons to follow their orders and to join with the Russian army before Smolensk. Despite their father's instructions they spent the month of August in camp at the mouth of the Dnieper River. At the beginning of September they advanced and during the following weeks they inflicted terrible devastation, especially in Galicia and Volhynia. The Tatars then swept across the southern part of Poland, reaching as far west as Cracow. But they made no attempt to join with Dmitri's army. Their reason, as was subsequently explained, was that they were anxious to avoid the heavily wooded regions of the north. The Tatars were accustomed to the steppelands where they could freely ride their small sturdy horses, attacking suddenly and as swiftly vanishing into the horizon. They had a deep mistrust of forests where they could be ambushed and thwarted in their traditional tactics.

This Tatar expedition nevertheless gave Ivan valuable support, although he was angry and disappointed that it failed to carry out his plan of directly helping in the capture of Smolensk. Alexander had been at Novgorodok when he had learnt that the Russians were laying siege to Smolensk. He had immediately made preparations to lead his army to defend this important stronghold. But then he had received news of the Tatar invasion and had decided to advance against them. Thus Ivan, at a time when he could ill afford them, was saved the necessity of sending reinforcements to his army at Smolensk, as he had undertaken to do in the event of Alexander marching to help the garrison.

Ivan's campaign of the summer of 1502 failed in its main purpose. In December, however, he ordered three armies to invade Lithuania, but this winter campaign was on a smaller scale and designed to maintain the pressure on Lithuania rather than to achieve important objectives. In any case neither the course of these operations nor their results are known.

Alexander had been spared further defeats at the hands of the Russians during 1502. He knew, however, that he could not count on such good fortune continuing with him. The annihilation of the Golden Horde meant that the Crimean Tatars were now free to despoil Lithuania and Poland, whose troops would be engaged in holding back the armies of Ivan. He recognized, too, that Lithuania could not withstand further Muscovite invasions and, although he was now their King, he could not count on help from the Poles. He was, therefore, more anxious than ever to make peace with Ivan, for if the war dragged on he would surely lose Smolensk, Kiev, and, in fact, the whole of Kievan Russia which Ivan was claiming as part of his patrimony.

During 1502 Alexander had twice made attempts to negotiate with his enemies. In July he sent messages to the Crimean Khan, proposing a peace treaty and suggesting that he might well be prepared to pay annual tribute. He proposed to send Dmitri Putyatich whom he had sent on a previous occasion to discuss the proposition further. But Mengli-Girei merely sent Alexander's letter to Ivan. He himself did not trouble to reply, especially as at this time his two younger sons were ravaging the southern parts of both Lithuania and Poland.

The approach to Ivan was by means of a letter from the *pans* or nobles of the Lithuanian Council to the Boyar Council in Moscow. Proposing peace the Lithuanian nobles requested safe-conducts so that their representatives could come to negotiate. This message reached Moscow towards the end of August, when Dmitri's army was beginning its siege of Smolensk and the Crimean Tatars were invading Lithuania. It was a time when Ivan was confident of the successful outcome of his campaign, but he did not reject the offer to negotiate and sent the safe-conducts.

The ambassador who arrived in Moscow at the end of December [1502] to conduct the first stage of the negotiations was Sigismund Santay, who came from Vladislav, King of Hungary and Bohemia and brother to Alexander. Santay at his first audience with Ivan on 1 January [1503] presented a letter from Pope Alexander VI who called on him to join in a great crusade against the infidel Turks. But Ivan, who had eagerly sought alliance with the Sultan and counted on the Crimean Khan as his closest ally, was not interested in proposals for such crusades. Santay then conveyed a message from Regnus, the papal legate in Hungary, calling on Ivan to stop hostilities against his son-in-law. The letter from Vladislav himself, read out to Ivan on the next morning, was even more unpalatable, for it bluntly called for an end to hostilities, the payment of compensation to Alexander for all damage caused by Russian aggression, and the return of all lands and prisoners seized. To this letter Ivan replied at length, justifying his actions and formally claiming as his patrimony not merely the lands which he had captured, but all the Russian lands in the possession of the Grand Prince of Lithuania. He stated, moreover, that he would continue to wage war until he had recovered them. But he was prepared to discuss terms for peace with Alexander.

The embassy from Poland–Lithuania, headed by Peter Myshkovsky and Stanislav Glebovich, and accompanied by Ivan Gildorp, representing the Master of the Livonian Order, reached Moscow in March

1503. Early in the negotiations they played what they believed to be the strongest card in their hands. This was a letter from Queen Elena, imploring her father to put an end to the war. The Roman Catholic bishops of Poland and King Alexander himself had undoubtedly called on her to make this appeal, but her letter was more than a plea written on such instigation or under duress. It was an impassioned, dignified, and moving defence by a wife of her husband who was, she insisted, both loving and tolerant and free of all blame for the cruel war ravaging the land of her adoption. She had not suffered persecution in any form, but worshipped freely in her faith. In every other particular her husband had observed the terms of the 1494 treaty and not he, but the Grand Prince, her father, was to blame for the war. She also sent letters to Sofia Palaeologa, her mother, and to Vasily and Yury, her brothers, begging them to influence her father to make peace.

Elena's letter must have come as a shock to Ivan. He had thought of her solely as his daughter and unwitting agent at the Lithuanian court and had not anticipated her loyalty to her husband and her new country. Also he had complained so frequently that she was being persecuted by Roman Catholic and Uniate bishops and denied freedom of worship that her furious denial of such charges was a major diplomatic reverse. But no matter how sincere and truthful her protestations might be, Ivan would never have accepted them, because they ran contrary to his policy. In fact, at the end of the negotiations he wrote sternly reproaching her for denying the truth in her letter, admonishing her to observe her faith, and warning her of the damnation she would suffer if she betrayed her faith and her country. He had either convinced himself that her letter was false, or he was himself guilty of a monumental display of hypocrisy.

In his reply on 10 March to the statement of Alexander's ambassadors delivered at their first audience, Ivan was again unyielding in his demands. All the territory which he had taken in the course of the war was part of his patrimony as was also the territory, still in Lithuanian possession, which was peopled by Orthodox Russians. If Alexander would not yield on these demands, the war would continue. But this was merely the beginning of the negotiations when each side stated its full demands and then prepared to make piecemeal concessions; the question was which side would be compelled to concede most towards the final compromise.

The negotiations having reached deadlock, Alexander's ambassador retired for discussions with the Hungarian, Santay, who had taken no part so far, but had waited patiently in the background. On 15 March Santay was received in audience in the Kremlin. He had no real proposals to offer, but evidently hoped to impress Ivan with the information that an envoy from the Sultan was already in Vilna. He was, Santay asserted, negotiating an alliance with Alexander which would bode ill for Muscovy if the Grand Prince continued his hostilities. But then, incongruously, Santay delivered an impassioned appeal to Ivan to make peace with Alexander and to join him in a crusade against the Turks. Again Ivan was not impressed. He did not believe that the Sultan would make any agreement, still less an alliance, with Alexander. His reply was a stubborn demand for the cession of all the lands that he claimed.

Negotiations were resumed on 17 March [1503]. Alexander's ambassadors and the Hungarian then made a proposal, intended to break the deadlock. They suggested that a truce should be signed to allow both parties to work out a compromise. This suited Ivan who, with every appearance of reluctance, finally approved a truce for six years, during which period all the towns and lands seized by the Russians would remain in his full and legal possession.

The truce provided that during this six-year period, ending on 15 March 1509, Alexander would send his ambassadors to negotiate a permanent peace. Until this came about, however, all the territory gained by the Russians would be part of the realm of the Russian Grand Prince. But Ivan regarded these acquisitions as permanent and he could take pride in their extent, for they represented much of the territory that he had set out to recover. They embraced a vast area east of the Dnieper River and spreading west to include the whole basin of the Seym as well as the Desna River with the important regions of Novgorod Seversky and, farther to the west, Chernigov, and to the north Trubchevsk, Starodub, and Bryansk would all be absorbed into Muscovy. In the north the districts of Toropets and the principalities of the Belsky, Shemyachich, and Mozhaisky joined with Vyazma in coming under Moscow's rule. Her frontier, in fact, had moved a great distance to the west. But Vitebsk, Smolensk, and Mstislavl now formed a Lithuanian bulge which Ivan could not accept and, indeed, the failure to recover Smolensk rankled with him as a major disappointment. However, Smolensk was now only some thirty miles from his frontier and Kiev, his other great objective, was readily accessible from his new possessions on the Desna River.

The Livonian envoy had remained in the background throughout the negotiations, virtually ignored by the Russians. It was the established custom that the Master of the Livonian Order could negotiate with the

Grand Prince only through his officials in Novgorod and Pskov. The Livonian representative now asked that he might agree a truce, similar to that signed with the Lithuanians, but directly with the Grand Prince himself. His request was unceremoniously rejected, and he was forced to negotiate in Novgorod.

The terms of the truce with Lithuania must have distressed Alexander. He had briefed his ambassadors to insist on the return of the lands seized by the Russians and, in fact, to cede no territory. At the same time he had instructed them to secure an end to hostilities at all costs. In the event they had had no alternative but to accept Ivan's terms and they probably felt that they had done well in securing agreement to a truce rather than a treaty. Alexander may have been expecting that Ivan would be more amenable to argument and more ready to compromise; if this was so, he gravely misunderstood the outlook and character of his father-in-law, for Ivan considered himself to be in an unassailable position in which he had no need to make concessions.

For his part, however, Alexander was not ready to accept the loss of such extensive territories to Moscow, and he certainly had no intention of converting the truce into a permanent peace. His ambassadors had on 2 April taken part in a solemn ceremony when they and the Muscovite representatives had sworn on the cross to honour the terms of the truce and especially not to renew hostilities. But Alexander very early showed that he did not propose to observe the truce, while Lithuanian lands remained in Muscovite possession, and that on a suitable opportunity he would renew hostilities.

Ivan also regarded the truce as a temporary expedient and no more. He had in a message to the Crimean Khan, soon after the solemn oaths confirming the agreement, explained that he had accepted it merely to allow his troops to rest and to consolidate his position along the new frontier with Lithuania. Indeed, notwithstanding the six-year truce, war between Muscovy and Lithuaina was soon imminent.

In May 1503 Ivan sent Peter Pleshcheev and Konstantin Zabolotsky to Vilna to witness the King's oath to observe the terms of the truce. They were also instructed to obtain the King's signature to a document guaranteeing Elena's freedom to worship in the Orthodox faith. Ivan had emphasized this matter early in April in Moscow during the formal ceremony there and it was evident that he was planning to use his daughter's faith again as a pretext for war.

Ivan's intention to renew and continue hostilities against Lithuania was revealed clearly in his relations with Mengli-Girei in this period. The truce had made no difference to his policy towards the Khan. As before, he was counting on the Tatars to attack Lithuania and Poland at every opportunity. The more they devastated the lands of his enemy, weakening and demoralizing the people, the better it suited Ivan who would himself attack when the time was ripe.

The truce with Alexander nevertheless complicated his relations with Mengli-Girei. The first difficulty was that the Tatars, accustomed to raiding Lithuanian territory, did not take count of the fact that large areas had now come into Muscovite possession. In 1503, for example, Tatar bands raided the lands of the Seym River which were no longer part of Lithuania. From Moscow protests were made to the Khan, but small-scale raids continued.

Ivan's main problem at this juncture, however, was to retain Mengli-Girei as his ally, encouraging him to continue his aggression against Lithuania, while explaining away his truce with Alexander by which he had sworn to make no attacks on him for six years. On the eve of negotiations with Alexander's ambassadors in Moscow, Ivan had sent messages to Mengli-Girei urging him to invade Lithuania. Moreover, he had mentioned that he himself was planning a new campaign. In August 1503, not long after the truce was agreed, he had sent word to the Crimea that he was on the point of launching an expedition, led by his three sons, Vasily, Yury, and Dmitri, and urging the Khan to send his Tatars into southern Lithuania. The Muscovite army did not march, however, and Ivan's references to aggressive plans were evidently intended only to discourage the Khan from thinking that Ivan wanted an end to hostilities against Alexander.

More than four months passed before Ivan attempted to inform the Khan of his negotiations for peace with Lithuania. The message had been carried in August by the same envoy who was instructed to report that the new Muscovite campaign was about to be launched, led by Ivan's sons. Ivan lied and distorted the facts grossly in his attempt to retain his ally with his policy of aggression undiminished. But after the actual signing of the truce it became unavoidable the explain the position fully. In September [1503] Ivan sent Ivan Oshcherin to inform the Khan about it. In private audience he was to tell the Khan that a five, not six, year truce had been concluded and that Ivan had agreed to it solely on the condition that Alexander made a similar truce with the Khan. Oshcherin was instructed also to do all in his power to prevent the institution of diplomatic exchanges between Alexander and Mengli-Girei, and he was to impress upon the Khan that Alexander was a treacherous ally, not to be trusted at any time.

On their arrival, Alexander's ambassadors to the Crimean Khan adopted a threatening attitude, contrasting with the rather placatory tone of previous approaches. The reason for the change was the Shaikh Ahmad, the former Khan of the Golden Horde, had fallen into the hands of Alexander who hoped to use him to bargain. His ambassadors proposed to Mengli-Girei a peace on the terms that had been agreed between their fathers, Haji-Girei and Casimir, and that, if this could not be accepted, Alexander would set up Shaikh Ahmad as a rival Tatar ruler.

This threat did not greatly intimidate the Khan. Also the prospect of a treaty of peace with Alexander held far less attraction for him than his alliance with Ivan which had proved so profitable and which in September 1504 he confirmed. Already he was actively planning new campaigns in which Ivan was to join with the object of taking Kiev and ultimately of dismembering Lithuania. Thus Ivan had succeeded in his diplomacy in holding Mengli-Girei as his ally, unwavering in his hostility to Lithuania. He had succeeded equally in preventing an agreement or understanding between Alexander and the Khan. Meanwhile he was observing the truce and would continue to observe it for just as long as it suited him.

In fact, the six-year truce which Ivan and Alexander had sworn solemnly in April and May 1503 to observe brought no peace between them. To Ivan it was no more than a convenient break in hostilities, and Alexander did not accept its terms as lasting. Their attitudes infected their peoples. Fighting did not cease, but for a time it changed in character. Instead of massive armies advancing, local bands raided over the frontier. The war of 1500–03 was merely a stage in a longer struggle, and war could have broken out afresh at any time. But Ivan and Alexander both died before they could embark on the next stage of their struggle.

Chapter Twelve

The Administration of Muscovy

THROUGHOUT his long and extremely active reign of nearly forty-four years, Ivan was faced with pressing internal problems. The absorption of the principalities which had been independent or under Lithuanian rule was more than a matter of conquest and annexation. It was further necessary to integrate them so that their administration and their fiscal and judicial practices were coordinated with those of the rest of the realm.

This was a complex process and Ivan handled it with his usual caution. Newly annexed principalities were often allowed to keep their own regional systems of administration for a time. Ivan appointed his own governor and the regional administration worked to him, instead of to the former ruler; subject to this difference, the regional authorities enjoyed considerable autonomy. But gradually the Muscovite system was being applied throughout Muscovy and Great Russia. In the process the Muscovite forms of government and administration, which had been adequate to the needs of a small principality, had to change and be adapted to the problems of the vast new nation. This task was not properly tackled until the 1550s when Ivan III's grandson, Ivan the Terrible, guided by a group of outstanding advisers, embarked on a series of important reforms.

In the 15th century the administration in Muscovy

comprise two branches, the state and palace systems. The palace administration was concerned with the special guard of the Grand Prince as well as the running of his private estates and other special departments such as his stables, his falconry, the provision of food for the palace, and similar functions. This was the private administration of the Grand Prince, which because his estates and wealth were so great rivalled the state administration in importance for a time.

The state administration dealt with the collection of tribute, formerly gathered by the officers of the Great Khan, and which was still levied by the Grand Princes even after they had ceased paying it to the Horde. This branch of the administration was also responsible for the courts and the execution of justice, and for the conscription of troops. In the provinces the officers, appointed by the Grand Prince to be responsible for the state administration, were the *namestniki* [governors or lieutenants] and the *volosteli* [district chiefs], the former being in charge in towns and the latter in rural districts. The Grand Prince paid these officials no allowance or salary. They derived their income from the town or rural district in their charge. They were permitted to keep for themselves part of the court fees and the taxes which they collected, and they levied food and other goods from the people in amounts fixed by custom. This system, whereby officials lived off or fed themselves from the land was known as *kormlenie* [lit. feeding]. In the hands of corrupt and ruthless officials the system gave rise to serious abuses, and the people in towns and rural districts came to hate these officials who preyed on them. The abolition of *kormlenie* was to be one of the most important reforms carried out or at least started by Ivan the Terrible.

Difficulties arose in the administration of newly annexed territories in which the people had had no experience of Muscovite practices. Early in his reign Ivan III found it necessary to enact charters, regulating the obligations of such people to his officials and himself. The charters were necessary not only to define liabilities, but also to protect the people from extortion under the *kormlenie* system.

The full text of the charter, granted by Ivan III to the people of Beloozero in 1488, has survived and it is an important source of material on mediaeval Russian administrative practice. The principality of Beloozero had belonged to Prince Mikhail of Vereya, who had, as related in the next chapter, bequeathed it to his Grand Prince. On his death in 1486 Ivan had sent officials to study the local practices and the changes needed to integrate the region as a province of Muscovy, and this charter had resulted from their reports. It provided the procedure for the arrest and trial of criminals, and established the amount of the payments due to local officials, payable twice yearly, at Xmas and on St Peter's Day. The people paid their contributions to their own elected representatives, not directly to the officials. In court proceedings the presiding judge was obliged to consult with the men elected locally, and the people in the towns and rural districts could make complaints against their officials, even to the extent, it seems, of making formal representations to the Grand Prince himself.

Inevitably, however, the regional charters perpetuated local customs, even if only in modified form, and so were not satisfactory in a united country, except as a temporary arrangement. A single charter applicable to the whole nation was needed, and in 1497 this was promulgated in the form of the *Sudebnik* or legal code. It was probably prepared by a special committee, appointed by Ivan, under the chairmanship of Prince Ivan Patrikeev. But it was in many of its sections based on the ancient Russian code, known as the *Russkaya Pravda* [Russian justice], belonging to the Kievan period, and on the Pskov charters of the 14th and 15th centuries.

The *Sudebnik* was primarily concerned with the basic procedure and principles to be observed by the superior and local courts. The three higher courts mentioned are the Supreme Court, the Boyar Court, and the Court of Limited Jurisdiction. The Supreme Court, from which no appeal lay, was composed of boyars and state secretaries, sitting under the chairmanship of the leader of the Boyar Council. The Boyar Court investigated matters and reported to the Grand Prince who delivered the final judgment. The Court of Limited Jurisdiction, presided over by a boyar or state secretary appointed specially for each case, reported its decisions to the Supreme Court for approval. In towns and rural districts the Grand Prince's officials, known as *Kormlenshchiki*, because they were maintained by the *kormlenie* or "feeding" system, administered justice. But the *Sudebnik* also contained the provision, set out in the Beloozero Charter, that representatives of the local people should take part in the court proceedings.

The legal principles, laid down in the *Sudebnik* were evidently intended to guide the courts rather than to provide a full and binding statement of the law. Among the matters covered were scales of punishments for various crimes, litigation concerning landed estates, merchants' loans, disputes between employers and employees, and between landlords and peasants, and slavery. Article 9, reflecting the new power of the Grand Prince, provided the death penalty for major state crimes and specifically for armed rebellion and sedition against the sovereign. It is of particular interest that for such crimes the *Sudebnik* decreed the death penalty, for the *Russkaya Pravda* had made no provision for capital punishment. In Novgorod and Pskov such penalty had been part of the law and, indeed, Muscovite Grand Princes had in the 14th and 15th centuries had traitors executed, but the *Sudebnik* of 1497 specified the death penalty for the first time in Great Russia.

Article 57 regulated the right of the peasants to move from the estates of their landlords and to migrate freely. This right was in the following century to be curtailed and peasants were to be tied to the land and to their landlords, thus bringing to birth the evil system of serfdom. This article of the *Sudebnik* confirmed the rights of the peasant to move, but it provided that they could exercise this right only during the two weeks around 26 November, "the autumn St George's Day", the date by which traditionally the harvest had been gathered. At this time the peasant could settle any debts owed by him and also pay his taxes due to the Grand Prince. Further provisions governed the payments to be made by peasants, living in houses provided by the landlords. The article was evidently intended not to suppress the peasant's right to depart, but to regulate it in the interest of all concerned, including the Grand Prince, who required that his taxes be paid and that the harvests should not rot in the fields through lack of labour to gather it.

In the 15th century the political and administrative union of Great Russia was developing rapidly, but certain divisions remained. These divisions were primarily social and economic, based on the system of landownership, and were so deep-rooted that they persisted for many years to come. The main categories of land at this time were (1) state lands, (2) the lands of the Grand Prince, (3) the patrimonial estates of the lesser princes, which they retained after surrendering their independence and becoming the serving princes of the Grand Prince, (4) boyar lands which included all privately owned land, and (5) church and monastery lands.

The serving princes and boyars, possessing patrimonial estates, were the chief danger to the authority of the Grand Prince. The regional charters and the *Sudebnik* itself, which were important steps towards providing a single administrative and judicial system for the whole country, did not apply to the patrimonial estates or to the church and monastery lands. The serving princes, even after swearing allegiance to the Grand Prince, continued to exercise their traditional authority over the people within their estates. It was to Ivan III an anomaly that these princes and their domains should stand outside his authority and an affront to his policy of the complete unification of the country. But he proceeded cautiously, making no direct attack on these patrimonial immunities. His remedy was to establish landholding based on service, creating the *posmetie* in place of the patrimonial estate, the *votchina*.

Lands belonging to the church and to monasteries enjoyed even greater autonomy and immunity from his laws. Since the days of Kievan Russia, the church had had special privileges. Vladimir's Church Statute had made "church people", a term embracing not only churchmen but all laymen with their families who directly served the church and worked its lands, subject not to the Grand Prince, but to the Metropolitan. The Mongols had given the church special charters of immunity. Churches and monasteries had added to their estates, while retaining all their special privileges. Church people and landed estates of the church were exempt from taxation and had no liability for military service. In the 14th and 15th centuries the church had called on the Grand Princes to confirm these privileges, but while it had obtained the confirmation, it had found the Christian princes far less sympathetic and amenable than the Mohammedan Khans. The charters, issued by the Grand Princes, had continued the administrative and judicial immunity of the church, but had made the peasants on church lands liable for taxes. Nevertheless the vast estates of the church and the exemption of its people from military service were to prove increasingly unacceptable to Ivan III, as he struggled against his enemies and unified his country.

The great need at this time was for a centralized military organization, and this was not something which could be erected suddenly. But Ivan III took important steps towards creating the new class of gentry who could serve as the core of such an organization. The army on which Ivan III depended was based on his personal corps, known as his *dvor*, supplemented by members of the lower gentry, the boyars' sons as they were called, serving under his command or the command of the *voevoda*, appointed by him. His brothers and the serving princes all with their personal troops rallied to the summons of the Grand Prince. In addition he could mobilize merchants and citizens in Moscow and other towns as well as enlisting Tatar and Cossack forces. All of these troops were mounted, except for the townsmen who served as infantry.

The Grand Prince also had the power to order a general conscription, but in practice this applied only in time of great crisis. Dmitri Donskoi had ordered such a conscription throughout Muscovy in 1380, as had his son, Vasily I, in 1396. But the success of such conscriptions depended too much on the zeal and co-operation of all princes, boyars, and citizens for it to serve as a reliable means of providing an army.

As Ivan III's need for troops increased and as he absorbed the manpower of the territories which he annexed, he concentrated more on building up the class of serving gentry. This class served him directly and was more dependable politically than the princes and boyars with their private retinues. The serving gentry, therefore, provided an important element in the centralization of the army. But the problem, so difficult to solve, was the maintenance of the gentry, for the Grand Prince lacked the finances to pay them. The only method was to grant them estates, to be held on service tenure, but this faced him with the scarcity of land, suitable and available for the purpose.

Most of Muscovy was still forest land. The comparatively small areas which had been cleared, were cultivated by peasants who by custom had certain rights in the land they worked. Moreover they paid taxes which provided much-needed revenue. For this reason Ivan would not readily disturb their lands. Nor was he ready to carve up the palace lands into estates for the serving gentry, because they produced goods and income for the maintenance of himself and his establishment.

The two remaining categories—the patrimonial estates of the princes and boyars and the land belonging to the church and monasteries—embraced vast areas from which the needs of the new class of gentry could readily be met. Ivan was not prepared at this stage to encroach on the patrimonial estates of the princes and boyars. They were still a powerful class, on whose members he depended to fill all high offices of state and to command his armies. Moreover, their patrimonial rights were entrenched by tradition. He did not hesitate, however, to take over the lands of princes and boyars who were guilty of treason.

In the new territories which he seized, Ivan did not

feel the same need to observe local traditions. After the final subjugation of Novgorod in 1477 he gradually dispossessed the boyar class which had opposed him. In 1489 alone 9,000 Novgorod boyars as well as small landholders and merchants were deported and replaced by a similar number of Muscovite boyars, gentry, and merchants. It is calculated that by 1500 he had acquired by confiscation in the Novgorod region about 2,700,000 acres of land, most of which he granted to members of the gentry class. This large-scale resettlement is of special interest, because Ivan did not grant any new estates on a freehold, full-ownership basis. All were *pomestie* or military fiefs in which occupation was conditional on the rendering of service to the Grand Prince.

A large part of the Novgorod land which Ivan seized had belonged to the church. He had felt able to take drastic action in this case because churchmen had been among those plotting treason against him. He could not take similar direct action against the church in Muscovy where it held great estates. Here, most of all, he needed land to settle members of the gentry, where they could be expeditiously mobilized with their men to meet attacks by Tatars and other enemies. The secularization of church and monastery lands would have solved the problem of providing the gentry with estates, and at one stage it even seemed that the ownership of land and other wealth would be condemned by the church itself.

The Russian Orthodox Church had freed itself from the authority of the Patriarch of Constantinople and had become the national Russian church. From this had arisen the special relationship of the Grand Princes to the church. He was its protector and, since his approval was necessary to the appointment of the Metropolitan, he wielded great authority in church affairs. Moreover, an impassioned dispute broke out towards the end of Ivan III's reign which, it seemed, would strengthen his resolve to secularize at least part of the church lands. This dispute was between two factions within the church, the Trans-Volga Hermits and the Josephans. The former followed the teachings of Nil Sorski that the church must reject luxury and the possession of property so that its priests and monks could dedicate themselves to prayer and meditation. The Josephans, so called after the renowned abbot of Volokolamsk monastery, maintained that the church needed its wealth and the protection of the state to carry out its great mission among the people. Both factions had strong support among the princes and boyars. Several heresies which arose at this time, and especially the heresy of the Judaizers, referred to in the next chapter, also opposed landowning by the church. But Ivan moved cautiously. The Josephans, who believed in the church retaining its estates, were strong upholders of the authority of the Grand Princes; they represented the long tradition of church support for the unification of Russia under the rule of Moscow. The Trans-Volga Hermits, preaching a return to monasticism and detached from worldly affairs, offered no such support. In the event the Josephans carried the day in the church councils. Ivan, while anxious to obtain the church lands, was even more anxious to avoid a direct conflict with the church and he could not afford to sacrifice its powerful support. Secularization of ecclesiastical lands was to remain an important issue for many decades to come and, indeed, only in 1764, over 250 years later, was the final secularization of the bulk of the church estates decreed.

Chapter Thirteen

The Apanage Principalities and the Dynastic Crisis of 1497–99

URING the first twenty-eight years of his reign
Ivan met with no real opposition among his
people. The only internal challenge came from his
brothers, Prince Andrei of Uglich and Prince Boris
of Volok, and their rebellion of 1480 had faced him
with what was probably the most serious domestic
crisis of his reign. To Ivan this had been not merely
a problem of the personal rivalry of his brothers, but
of the apanage princes whose principalities were in
many respects like independent states. Within such
principalities the Grand Prince had no jurisdiction
and he could claim the loyalty and obedience of the
apanage princes only in matters beyond their frontiers, such as relations with other parts of the country
or with foreign rulers or in war. The apanage princes
were thus potentially dangerous obstacles to the strong
centralized state which he was creating. He therefore
pursued a policy of limiting the power of these princes,
reducing them to the simple status of subjects, and of
finally absorbing their estates. But he had to proceed
gradually, for the idea of the apanage principality was
too deeply rooted in Russian life, and the princes themselves were too influential, to be destroyed suddenly
and dramatically.

After their rebellion of 1480 Ivan's two brothers,

Prince Andrei and Prince Boris, had come to terms with him and had returned to their principalities. But their continued independence could not fail to make him uneasy. At a critical juncture in his diplomacy they had threatened him with civil war and had even tried to negotiate with the enemy. He knew that they were capable of repeating such treasonable conduct and of endangering his throne and the country. Ivan's grandson, Ivan the Terrible, and even his son, Vasily III, would have taken strong action to eliminate these dangers. He himself may have felt that he had not yet acquired the power and authority to deal so forthrightly with the apanage princes. But in any case he preferred more subtle tactics, avoiding open conflict so far as possible.

Ivan had made treaties with his two brothers soon after the crisis between them over the estate of Prince Yury. His next step was to begin discussion on the revision of these treaties, and it was by such revisions that he diminished their rights and privileges. The revised treaties, agreed in February 1481, bound Andrei and Boris to accept as part of the patrimony of the Grand Prince not only the estate of Prince Yury, which he had seized, but also Novgorod and all of her possessions. In return Ivan conceded certain unimportant lands to them. At this time, too, Ivan succeeded in persuading his youngest brother, Prince Andrei of Vologda, to bequeath his estate to him. A few months later Andrei conveniently died and Ivan acquired his principality. In 1485 he annexed the whole of the grand principality of Tver, apparently without reference to his brothers who could only stand by, impotently watching the aggrandizement of their brother's possessions.

Next to be absorbed by Ivan was the apanage principality of Vereya. Prince Mikhail of Vereya, a first cousin of Vasily II and grandson of Dmitri Donskoi, had supported Vasily II throughout the struggle for the throne waged by the other descendants of Dmitri Donskoi. His reward for this loyalty had been the grant of lands in addition to confirmation that he could retain his patrimonial estate of Vereya, situated to the south of Mozhaisk, and the northern principality of Beloozero. Within these principalities he exercised the same full and independent power that Ivan's brothers wielded in their principalities, and it was galling to Ivan that there were such further parts of his realm where he had no jurisdiction.

By nature Prince Mikhail was neither rebellious nor ambitious, and he was always ready to comply with Ivan's wishes. He and his sons served with their troops when called upon and they did not question their orders. Once in 1478, however, Prince Mikhail became involved in a quarrel among senior churchmen and on this occasion he may have incurred Ivan's displeasure, but this had no bearing on his ultimate fate. From the beginning of his reign Ivan set out to curtail his powers and finally to annex his principality. In 1482 he prevailed on Prince Mikhail to make him sole beneficiary under his will. In the following year he took advantage of a family misunderstanding to dispossess both Prince Mikhail and his son.

On the birth of Ivan's grandson, Dmitri, the first child of his son, Ivan Ivanovich, and his wife, Elena Stepanova, Ivan decided to reward the mother by presenting to her certain jewellery which had formed part of his first wife's dowry. He had entrusted or given these jewels to his own second wife, Sofia Palaeologa. She had bestowed some of them on her penurious brother, Andrei Palaeologus, and others on her niece, Maria, on the occasion of her marriage to Prince Vasily of Vereya. Ivan raged when he learned this. He at once sent officers to seize the jewellery and to arrest Prince Vasily and his wife. Warned of their impending arrest and believing themselves to be in disgrace, they fled over the frontier and sought asylum in Lithuania. There may well have been other reasons for this flight, but they are not known. However, their panic played into the hands of Ivan who promptly had Prince Vasily disinherited as a traitor. He compelled Prince Mikhail to make another agreement with him by which he swore to have no contact with his son and undertook to hold his patrimonial estates of Yaroslavets and Vereya merely on life tenure. On his death in 1486 his possessions were absorbed into the principality of the Grand Prince.

In dealing with his two remaining brothers, however, Ivan had to proceed more cautiously. Prince Boris was, in fact, to cause him no further anxiety until his death in 1494. Boris's two sons, Feodor and Ivan, were equally manageable, and Ivan soon acquired a large part of their possessions. But Prince Andrei of Uglich was more dangerous and he watched uneasily for this brother's next move against him. At one stage rumours circulated that he was about to flee to Lithuania. The rumours proved false and, since Andrei and his troops were active during the years 1487–89 in raiding over the Lithuanian border, Ivan had no grounds for acting against him. At this time, moreover, he was seeking to attract Orthodox Russians in Lithuania to transfer their allegiance to him and a false move against his own brother might well have discouraged them from taking such a step.

In the summer of 1491, however, Andrei played into Ivan's hands. Mengli-Girei had sent word to Moscow that the Golden Horde, supported by Nogay Tatars, was advancing to attack the Crimea after which they would turn north to invade Muscovy. In response to the Khan's appeal for help Ivan in June 1491 ordered his army, including the troops of his two brothers, to march to the south. Andrei refused to serve or to send his troops, but his reasons are not known. In September he went to Moscow where Ivan received him with every courtesy and then had him arrested. His two sons were imprisoned in Pereyaslavl. Two years later Andrei died in prison and his principality was annexed.

Ivan had thus by patient ruthless action seized all the apanage principalities, bestowed by his father on his brothers and his cousin. The sole exception was part of Prince Boris's principality and this he could take at any time. Moreover he had greatly weakened the tradition of the independence of such principalities, and by doing so had helped towards removing a major obstacle to the creation of a strong unified state with all power centralized in the hands of the Grand Prince or Tsar of all Russia.

In the 1480s, however, Ivan found himself faced with more extensive opposition than that of the apanage princes. It was certainly not strong or organized in a way to threaten his authority, but it found a point of focus and drew unexpected strength at this time from the dynastic crisis which clouded these years of his reign.

The dynastic crisis arose from the rivalry between Ivan's grandson, Prince Dmitri Ivanovich, and his son, Prince Vasily Ivanovich, for the succession. It became a complex struggle because of the strong characters of the mothers concerned and because of the opposition groups which rallied behind them. Unfortunately the gaps in the information of this period are so considerable that no full account of the crisis can be given and explanations of these events can only be largely conjectural.

By his first wife, Princess Maria of Tver, Ivan had

had a son, Ivan Ivanovich, known as Ivan Molodoi, whom he had come to treat as his heir to the throne and co-ruler, bearing the title of Grand Prince. Maria had died in 1467 and five years later Ivan had married Sofia Palaeologa. In January 1483 his son, Ivan Ivanovich, married Elena Stepanova, the daughter of Stephen IV of Moldavia, and she came to live with her husband in the Kremlin palace. To Sofia this was an unwelcome arrival, because the children of Ivan Ivanovich, the eldest son of the Grand Prince, would compete with her own sons for the succession to the throne of Muscovy. By the time of Elena's arrival in Moscow, Sofia had already borne three daughters and three sons [Vasily in March 1479, Yury in March 1480, and Dmitri in October 1481]. Sofia no doubt hoped that Elena would prove barren, but if so she was disappointed, for ten months after her arrival in Moscow Elena gave birth to a son, named Dmitri.

The birth of this grandchild apparently delighted Ivan far more than the birth of his own sons by Sofia. It was a fact that she cannot have failed to notice, and her bitterness towards Elena must have been intensified by the angry scenes over the jewellery which Ivan demanded from her for Elena. The humiliation of this incident undoubtedly further inflamed Sofia's feelings towards her stepson and his family. When in 1490 Ivan Ivanovich died of gout, rumour held that Sofia had poisoned him.

The rivalry between Sofia and Elena centred on the succession, now became acute. The question was who should be proclaimed heir—Vasily, Ivan III's eldest son by his second son, Sofia, or Dmitri, his grandson, the son of Ivan Ivanovich by his wife, Elena Stepanova. Ivan made no haste to declare his choice. Relations between the two women became more embittered. Around them formed two factions which have been the subjects of numerous theories and conjectures, and which were further complicated by religious antagonisms, concerned mainly with the heresy of the Judaizers.

This heresy apparently began in Novgorod in 1470. The anti-Muscovite party there had summoned Prince Mikhail Olelkovich, a Lithuanian prince, to help them in their struggle against the pro-Muscovite party. A member of the retinue of Olelkovich, a Jew named Skharia, began propagating a new faith, akin to Judaism, which quickly won supporters among the Novgorodtsi. The tenets of this heresy are not known, but it was undoubtedly opposed to many Orthodox dogmas and critical of the Orthodox hierarchy. The fact that it spread rapidly suggests that there was much popular dissatisfaction with the church at this time and especially with the wealthy monasteries. It also served as a means of protest by malcontents within both church and state. But the most important support that it gained at this stage was from the Grand Prince himself.

Ivan saw in this heresy a weapon which might help him to take possession of some, if not all, of the vast estates belonging to the church. He needed land, for despite the great expanse of his realm and despite the new lands which he had recovered from Lithuania, he was already hard pressed to provide estates for the rapidly growing class of serving gentry. This new class was assuming wider responsibilities and taking the place of the princes and boyars in providing the officers, both military and civil, on whom the Grand Prince increasingly relied in the task of consolidating and ruling the new centralized state.

This need for land to enfeoff the serving gentry was to become more acute during the following century. Ivan's successors also looked enviously at the church estates, but like him they did not dare sacrifice the support of the church by secularizing its lands. Evidently Ivan saw in this heresy of the Judaizers a possible means of discrediting the hierarchy and enabling him to secularize church property without thereby ranging the full opposition of the church against him. He had taken advantage of the disloyalty of Archbishop Feofil and other churchmen in Novgorod to secularize church lands there. No doubt he hoped that he might be able to take similar action in Muscovy as a whole.

The heresy apparently spread from Novgorod in 1479 when Ivan took with him to Moscow two priests, Alexei and Denis, who had been converted to the new teaching. Denis became priest of the Arkhangelsky Cathedral and Alexei became archpriest of the Uspensky Cathedral, both in the Kremlin, and their appointments carried considerable authority. Meanwhile the heresy was flourishing in Novgorod, unopposed by the church until the appointment at the end of 1484 of Gennady as Archbishop. In Moscow, too, the heresy spread without restraints. Several of the most important men at Ivan's court embraced it or were sympathetic towards it, including the *dyak* or state secretary, Feodor Kuritsyn, who was very influential. Archbishop Gennady, zealous in combating the heresy in Novgorod, in time carried the struggle into Moscow and it was primarily as a result of his pressure that Ivan felt compelled to convene a council in 1490 to consider measures to be taken against the heretics. This resulted in some curtailment of their activities, but the leaders, like Kuritsyn, continued to hold important positions.

Elena Stepanova at some stage embraced this heresy, which thus became a factor in the struggle over the succession. Ivan himself, who was tolerant towards it for secular rather than religious reasons, was also at this time indulgent towards Elena and her son, Dmitri, primarily because he was most anxious to cultivate the friendship of her father, Stephen of Moldavia, his ally against Lithuania. He was therefore unwilling to listen to those who criticized Elena for her heresy. His wife, Sofia, was foremost among Elena's enemies and in this she probably had the support of the church hierarchy and of many boyars. This party would have favoured the proclamation of Vasily, Sofia's son, as heir-apparent, while Elena's son, Dmitri, presumably had the support of Kuritsyn and other strongly placed heretics, as well as that of the serving gentry who as a whole opposed the boyars, and for reasons of domestic and foreign policy the sympathetic support of Ivan himself.

The death of Ivan Ivanovich, Ivan's eldest son, in 1490 marked the start of the crisis. There were no precedents to guide Ivan in choosing between his son and grandson and the decision lay with him alone. For seven years this crisis simmered beneath the surface of life in the Kremlin. Ivan made no move to decide who would be his successor. But he took great care to ensure that no suggestion of the bitter family antagonism should reach Lithuania. It was probably for this reason that he delayed making or announcing his decision. The proclamation of Vasily or Dmitri as his successor would give rise to opposition and probably the disgrace of members of the disappointed party. In either case it would arouse reactions beyond his frontiers which would hinder his policies.

Despite Ivan's care on this score, however, the crisis erupted in 1497. Sometime in that year Vasily, then aged eighteen, learnt from a certain Feodor Stromilov, a secretary in one of the departments, that his father was about to proclaim Dmitri as his successor with the title of Grand Prince of Vladimir and Moscow. Vasily and his mother, Sofia, brought together their supporters in a conspiracy to break away from the authority of Ivan. The plot was that Vasily would make his way to the northern provinces of Vologda and Beloozero, seize power there, and set up an independent principality. Dmitri was to be murdered.

Some evidence suggests that the supporters of Vasily and Sofia were opposed to Ivan's policy of establishing a strong centralized state. They favoured the old system of independent princes, linked in some form of federation. Vasily himself, however, was to show subsequently that he believed in a strong autocracy and he, in fact, did much to further his father's policy of creating a unified state. At this time, however, he may have been ready to seize on all support in a desperate attempt to secure an independent position from which to fight for the throne after his father's death.

Before Vasily, Sofia and their supporters could take any action, Ivan discovered their plot. He placed Vasily under arrest. He had six of his son's supporters beheaded on the ice of the Moskva River. Reports that "evil women" had been visiting Sofia with poisonous herbs, led to the arrest of several women, who were pushed through holes in the ice and drowned in the river. From that time, the chronicler of these events relates, Ivan lived with Sofia "in great vigilance".

With elaborate ceremonial on 4 February 1498 in the Cathedral of the Dormition in the Kremlin with the Metropolitan Simeon and the bishops officiating, Ivan blessed his grandson, Dmitri, who was crowned Grand Prince of Vladimir, Moscow, Novgorod, and all Russia. In taking this step of formally crowning his grandson Ivan's hand had undoubtedly been forced by the conspiracy of his wife and son. But again the main factor was probably political. An important stage in his plans against Lithuania had been reached. Stephen of Moldavia was one of his chief allies and the coronation of his grandson as successor to the throne of Muscovy would strengthen Stephen's support. But Ivan apparently underestimated the force of the reaction of Sofia and Vasily and their party. Meanwhile they were in disgrace and Ivan continued to take great pains that information concerning this family rivalry over the succession did not spread abroad, especially to Lithuania where it might undermine his diplomacy and discourage Orthodox Russians from changing their allegiance to Moscow.

Suddenly on 21 March 1499 Ivan publicly bestowed on Vasily the title of Grand Prince of Novgorod and Pskov. This meant that Vasily had been forgiven. But, although he had now received one of Dmitri's principalities, namely Novgorod, Dmitri remained the senior as "Grand Prince of all Russia", co-ruler and successor to the throne.

An upheaval at this time, involving several of the most eminent nobles and of Ivan's closest advisers, may have been connected with Vasily's return to favour. Prince Ivan Patrikeev, Prince Simeon Ryapolovsky, Prince Vasily Romodanovsky, and other leading boyars were evidently opposed to Ivan's foreign policy. After the subjugation of the Kazan Khanate in 1487, Ivan had turned westwards against Lithuania, intent on the reconquest of the Russian lands which he considered part of his patrimony. These boyars would have preferred a policy of friendship with Lithuania and continued war against the infidel Tatars and Turks. It has been suggested that Vasily and Sofia intrigued to influence Ivan against these boyars, especially Prince Ivan Patrikeev, who had been active against Vasily's supporters in 1497. According to this interpretation of these events Vasily and Sofia were opposed to the boyars and therefore supporters of the new class of serving gentry. Elena and Dmitri were assumed to lead the boyar party. The leading Russian historians, Karamzin, Solovyev, and Klyuchevsky, favoured this theory, which was based on the evidence of Kurbsky and others hostile to Sofia. More recent evidence suggests a reversal of these roles, so that Vasily and Sofia headed the boyar opposition to Ivan III's policies. But this connexion between these boyars and the plans laid by Vasily and Sofia is no more than conjecture.

In January 1499 Prince Ivan Patrikeev and his two sons, as well as Princes Vasily Ryapolovsky and Romodanovsky, were arrested. The Patrikeevs, saved by the intercession of the Metropolitan from execution, were compelled to become monks; Ryapolovsky was executed and Romodanovsky was imprisoned. A few weeks later Vasily and his mother were restored to favour, but this was only partial satisfaction of their demands. They could not rest until Vasily had supplanted Dmitiri as co-ruler and heir-apparent to the throne. In his determination to achieve this Vasily at once began plotting treason and flight. Sometime between September 1499 and September 1500 he fled to Vyazma, where his father's officers caught up with him and prevailed on him to return to Moscow. Probably Vasily intended this flight to embarrass his father at the critical time when he was preparing to march on Lithuania. Certainly Ivan now took great pains to satisfy his son's demands. On his return to Moscow Vasily was at once pardoned and even rewarded, for about this time he was granted the title of Grand Prince, which could only mean that he had succeeded in supplanting Dmitri. Formally Dmitri was still Grand Prince of Vladimir and Moscow, but on 11 April 1502 he and his mother were arrested and disgraced. Both were to perish, evidently by violence, Elena two years later and Dmitri in 1509. The dynastic crisis was at an end.

The family rivalry undoubtedly cast a cloud over Ivan's last years. Throughout his life he had impressed everyone by his self-mastery and restraint and now he appeared to falter. Under pressure from his wife and son he had ceded considerable powers to Vasily. He suffered rebuffs from the church council, probably supported by Vasily, in his plans to secularize church lands, and the severe punishment of heretics, which took place mainly as a result of the pressure of Archbishop Gennady, must have embittered him, for he had tolerated and even protected them. Herberstein reported that he was drinking heavily, regularly declining into a stupor after dinner. He had always been moderate in his habits. Contarini who had seen him several times some twenty years earlier bore witness to his restraint, especially in drinking, contrary to the habits of his people. Remorse and the strain of family rivalry had apparently in old age unnerved him. He died on 27 October 1505.

Chapter Fourteen

Ivan III's Successors:
Vasily III and Ivan IV

VASILY succeeded to the throne of Muscovy
without dispute on the death of his father,
Ivan III. The struggle for power between him and
his nephew, Dmitri, which many expected, did not
happen. As Vasily III he took the reigns of government firmly in his hands. Tall, slight in build, and
stooped, he resembled his father in appearance and
also to some extent in character. He had the same
tenacity of purpose, the same patience and ruthless-
ness. But he was more devout and energetic. He made
frequent pilgrimages to monasteries of special sanctity
and travelled extensively through his realm. Also he
was more ready to act decisively, although not always
more wisely, than his father, who had usually preferred
to rely on tortuous diplomacy.

Vasily devoted himself to carrying on the policy of
unifying the Russian lands under the central rule of
the Grand Prince of Moscow, but he did not find events
favouring him in the way that they had favoured his
father. Pskov, the part of Ryazan still independent,
and the remainder of the principality of Volok were
all incorporated into Muscovy without difficulty. But
the Kazan and Crimean Khanates now menaced Muscovy and their active hostility was a major handicap

to him as he sought to carry on the war against Lithuania.

Mohammed Amin, whom Ivan III had appointed and reappointed Khan of Kazan, had in the end revolted against Moscow's rule. Vasily in the spring of 1506 sent troops to reassert his authority, but they suffered two serious defeats at the hands of the Tatars. The situation along Muscovy's eastern frontier became dangerous, especially as the Grand Prince of Lithuania was now urging the Kazan Tatars to throw off the Muscovite yoke. In 1508, feeling himself to be insecure, Mohammed Amin approached Vasily with proposals for peace, but he died soon afterwards and trouble erupted again. Sahib Girei, brother of the Crimean Khan, became Khan of Kazan and this foreshadowed renewed Tatar action against Muscovy.

The key to the new Tatar challenge lay mainly in the changed policy of the Crimean Khan. Mengli-Girei had been Ivan's chief ally against Lithuania and the Golden Horde. But the Horde had been annihilated and Ivan's territorial gains from Lithuania had brought Moscow's frontiers too close to the Crimea for the liking of Mengli-Girei. Moreover, the lands on either side of the Dnieper River which the Crimean Tatars had so profitably plundered when part of Lithuania were now protected as being lands of an ally. A further factor, leading to the change in the Crimean Khan's policy, was the deterioration in relations between him and the Muscovite Grand Prince. Vasily failed to cultivate the goodwill of the Khan as assiduously as his father had done; in particular he refused to send rich presents, considering that this was the same as paying tribute, such as Muscovy had paid to the Great Khan for so many decades.

In 1512 Mengli-Girei formed an alliance with Sigismund, Grand Prince of Lithuania and King of Poland in succession to Alexander. He now had to refrain from raiding the Ukrainian lands belonging to his new ally, but he was free to send his troops into Muscovy. In 1521 Mohammed-Girei, the son and successor of Mengli, reached the outskirts of Moscow in one of his large-scale raids. The city, crowded with people seeking refuge from a cruel enemy and racked with disease, was saved only by costly presents to the Khan, who was virtually paid to raise the siege and withdraw his troops.

To Vasily the Tatars in the east, south-east, and south posed major problems. Ivan III had managed to keep them at bay by skilful diplomacy and during his reign Muscovy had not been seriously threatened by them. But Vasily suffered from their constant hostility. In the spring of each year he was compelled to send troops in force to man the lines of defence lying along the Oka River and to the strongholds erected south of this line. Also in these southern lands he settled companies of frontiersmen [*Ukrainniki*] to ward off Tatar attacks. But this annual despatch of troops proved a serious drain on Muscovite manpower. Moreover the distances were so great and the areas to be defended so immense that neither defence lines nor fortresses could ensure that Tatar raiding forces would not get through to the hinterland. It was therefore necessary to keep further Muscovite troops constantly in reserve.

Lithuania nevertheless remained the chief enemy. Ivan III had recovered extensive territories, but Smolensk and other important regions remained in Lithuanian hands. Furthermore Ivan III's gains had not been confirmed by treaty, but only by the unstable armistice of 1503. War broke out with Lithuania in 1508, when Vasily went to the aid of Prince Mikhail Glinsky, who had rebelled against Sigismund. Six years later Vasily mounted a full-scale invasion of Lithuania with the purpose of taking Smolensk. In this he was successful, but a few weeks later his army suffered a crushing defeat. He managed, however, to hold Smolensk against desperate Lithuanian attempts to recover it. When in 1522 he concluded a new armistice with Sigismund, this time for five years, he retained Smolensk as well as all the lands recovered earlier.

Throughout his reign Vasily, like his grandfather and father before him, was obsessed with the problem of the succession which was bound up with the continuance of the tradition of apanage princes. Ivan III had brought under his own rule all the apanage principalities granted by his father. He had, in fact, abolished the apanage system, but the tradition had survived with surprising strength, and he himself had felt compelled towards the end of his reign to bestow apanage principalities on his younger sons. By his will he bequeathed to Vasily virtually the whole principality, but granted small patrimonies to his other four sons. He admonished them as follows : "You, my children—Yuri, Dmitri, Simeon, Andrei—regard my son, Vasily, your eldest brother, as being in place of me, your father, and obey him in everything; and you, my son Vasily, treat your younger brothers with honour and without causing them offence."

In the past such testimentary instructions had not prevented family rivalries for power and Vasily regarded his brothers with deep suspicion. His first wife was barren and he worried all the more about the succession because his brothers inspired no confidence and Moscovy, surrounded by enemies, needed a strong Grand Prince. He married again and his second wife, Elena Glinskaya, gave birth on 30 August 1530 to a son, christened Ivan who was destined to rule as Tsar Ivan IV, "the Terrible". Another son, named Yuri, was born just over a year later. In 1533, however, Vasily fell mortally ill and his concern was that his son, Ivan, although then only three years old, should succeed. The danger was that his two surviving brothers, Princes Yuri and Andrei, would seize power from his young widow who, following Muscovite custom, would be regent during her son's minority.

Elena died suddenly after ruling for only five years as regent. Within that period, however, she had put down attempts by both Prince Yuri and Prince Andrei to seize power. A period of boyar anarchy followed after her death. It was a time of neglect and humiliation for Ivan and Yuri, both of whom went in fear of their lives. The experience of this period cut deeply into the mind and character of Ivan, developing in him characteristics which later made him notorious as "the Terrible". But this notoriety and the lurid legends of his reign have tended to obscure the fact that he was a great Tsar who advanced the policies of his father and grandfather with outstanding success.

The unification of Muscovy as a strong centralized state was finally achieved by Ivan IV. He did not forget the boyar rule of his childhood and, determined to eliminate opposition among the boyars to the supreme power of the Grand Prince, he crushed all signs of disaffection. In January 1547 he had himself crowned, not as Grand Prince, but as Tsar of all Russia. He thus carried to its completion the process, begun by his grandfather, of elevating the dignity and authority of the Grand Prince of Moscow far above all his princes, boyars, and subjects. Ivan III had used the title of Tsar of all Russia from time to time, but without the full significance given to it by Ivan IV who was the first Tsar to be crowned with the full title. The centralized state which was coming into being required a strong ruler whose power was beyond challenge, and

Ivan IV established the rule of the Tsar on that basis.

The Tatars continued to plague the new emergent nation and Ivan IV had first to deal with them before turning westwards. In 1552, after several abortive campaigns, he conquered Kazan and subjugated the khanate completely to his rule. A few years later he also conquered the khanate of Astrakhan. He had thus asserted Muscovite authority over the full length of the mighty Volga River. The colonization of the rich lands in the south and south-east, watered by the tributaries of the Volga and the Don, and to the east, beyond the Volga and into the expanses of Siberia could begin. The Russian people, while striving towards unity, were also impatient to expand in all directions and before the end of Ivan IV's reign the Stroganovs, a sturdy merchant family, had broken through into the Siberian lands.

The conquest of Kazan was one of the great events in Russian history. It was a victory which inspired legends. Since the time of Kievan Russia, the people had with a strong instinct moved towards unity. The division into trading-towns and then, in the upper Volga lands, into independent principalities had failed to give them the strength and security which they needed in the immense plain-lands where enemies surrounded them. Ivan III had expanded his realm and had united his people; he had, moreover, in 1480 finally freed them from the two-hundred-year yoke of the Tatars of the Golden Horde. But these achievements, although notable, had been undramatic and devoid of any real meaning for the people. The Russians were united by race, religion, geography, and by economic and political interest, but an inspiring event was needed to give birth to a popular sense of nationhood. The conquest of Kazan was such an event, and it might be said to have brought the nation to birth.

In the west, however, Ivan IV's policies had less success. He concentrated on the conquest of Livonia with the purpose of securing a permanent foothold on the shores of the Baltic Sea and of reviving Russian trade with the West. This policy brought him into conflict with the Swedes, the Teutonic Knights, and the Lithuanians and Poles. At first his military expeditions were successful, but then with the accession of Stefan Batory to the throne of Lithuania–Poland he suffered disastrous defeats. In the armistice for ten years, agreed in 1582, Ivan IV was forced to cede the whole of Livonia and certain other conquests to Stefan Batory, but he retained all the lands that had been recovered by his father and grandfather.

Within the reigns of three strong rulers—Ivan III, Vasily III, and Ivan IV—Great Russia had achieved unity and had emerged as a nation. The process had been rapid and, accompanied as it was by internal reforms and reorganization and constant war against the enemies who almost surrounded her, the nation needed a brief respite. More important than a respite, however, was the need for another strong Tsar to carry on the policy of unification and consolidation. Ivan IV had in a sudden fury killed his eldest son, who had given promise of being a ruler of the necessary calibre. Feodor, the son who succeeded, was simple-minded and unequal to the tasks of leadership. During his reign he left all government to his most able adviser, Boris Godunov, who was to succeed him as Tsar. But disputes over the succession weakened the nation at a time when strong rule was essential. Russia was plunged into the "Time of Troubles", as it is known in her history. Only with the election of Tsar Mikhail, the first of the Romanov dynasty, early in the 17th century, was the further development of Russia as a strong, united nation continued.

Appendix 1

THIS brief account of the role of the Varangians or Norsemen, based on the *Chronicle of "Nestor"*, has been generally accepted until recently. Soviet historians, in particular, now dismiss it as false. They maintain that the Varangians were invited to Russia to serve as a bodyguard for the princes, but apart from serving in this capacity they wielded neither power nor influence. They never merged with the Russian people or settled in Russian lands. Moreover, they appeared only when Kievan Rus already existed as a state and had fought successfully against nomadic invaders and even against Byzantium. Soviet historians further maintain that the *Ancient Chronicle*, on which the Varangian theory is based, was distorted and amended subsequently as a result of the rivalries between Novgorod and Kiev, and especially by the Novgorod chroniclers who were intent on minimizing the importance of Kiev.

Controversy will no doubt continue over this important chapter in Russian history. The chronicle may well have been corrupted as suggested, but the element of national pride and propaganda in Soviet denials of all foreign influence in the formation of the nation prompts the Western historian to regard this interpretation with some caution.

Appendix 2

CONFUSION exists in the use of the names "Mongol" and "Tatar", especially in referring to the great Asiatic invasions of the 13th century and subsequently to the Golden Horde and the other Khanates.

Until the late 12th century the main tribes of Mongolia were the Merkits, the Keraits, the Naimans, the Mongols, and the Tatars; there was no generic name embracing all of them. The Mongols became prominent in the middle of the century, but were soon afterwards almost annihilated by the neighbouring Tatars. Had it not been for the fact that the future conqueror, Chingiz or Genghiz Khan, was a Mongol, the name might have been lost to history. Chingiz Khan forged the new nation, known as "Mongol".

In Western Europe the Mongol invaders were all known as Tatars, or Tartars, and in Russia this name was retained. A great many of the troops serving in the Mongol armies during the great invasions were Turks, and the name Tatar was thus applied by the Russians to the Turkish tribes which were later centred mainly on the Crimea, Kazan, and Astrakhan.

In this study the invading hordes are given the name "Mongol", and the later Khanates are referred to as "Tatar".

Appendix 3

THE degree of influence exercised by Sofia on Ivan III, on Russian policy at this time, and indeed on the course of Russian history has been a matter of dispute among historians. In general her influence has been greatly exaggerated. For this the fault lies primarily with the enemies of her son and grandson, Vasily III and Ivan IV, who blamed her for their misfortunes. Prince Andrei Kurbsky, Ivan IV's antagonist, called her "a Greek sorceress" who wielded a strong and evil influence; he even held her guilty of poisoning her stepson, Ivan Molodoi, so that he would not stand in the way of the succession of her own son, Vasily III.

Russian historians in the 18th and 19th centuries ascribed to her a dominating influence. They asserted that Ivan III acquired the legal right to the Byzantine throne through his marriage with her, that the marriage gave rise to the theory of Moscow as the "third Rome", that she was responsible for the introduction of Byzantine court procedures into Moscow, that her advice and influence were responsible for the annexation of Novgorod and for the discarding of the Tatar yoke, and so forth.

S. M. Solovyev and V. O. Klyuchevsky, the two greatest Russian historians, discounted most of the theories of their predecessors. Both acknowledged, however, that she had exercised considerable influence in the development of the Muscovite court, in raising the dignity and prestige of the Grand Prince, and in encouraging Ivan to engage Italian architects and to erect impressive new buildings in his capital.

Historians in the 20th century have gone further in denying Sofia's influence, not only in the political developments of the time, but in every other way. Indeed Mr J. L. I. Fennell has held that Ivan III could have seen in her no more than an "exotic embellishment for his somewhat crude court" and that "there are no signs of Sofia's influence in the creation of a new court ceremonial or of new court ranks and functions".

Professor George Vernadsky, after summarizing the views of earlier historians, stated his conclusion that she could hardly have had any serious effect on state affairs, but that she must have influenced the court and the prestige of the Grand Prince. Moreover, she was undoubtedly instrumental through intrigue in ensuring the succession of her son, Vasily III. His final conclusion, however, was that "her main impact on the course of Russian history was made by the fact of her giving birth to the man who was destined to become the father of Ivan the Terrible".

To the present writer it seems an extreme view to deny to Sofia any influence whatsoever. The hostility of her contemporaries suggests that she was more than a mere "producer of heirs and an exotic embellishment" in Moscow. To them she was an enemy to be feared and respected. She had grown up in a city where women often wielded considerable influence, and she was undoubtedly an educated and astute woman with a mind of her own. The main course of Ivan III's policy was already clear before her arrival in Moscow and it cannot be said that she influenced him in the annexation of Novgorod, the throwing off of the Tatar yoke, or in his other policies. But she brought with her something of the prestige of Byzantium and the experience of Rome; she probably guided her husband in introducing a new grandeur and dignity to the court and capital; she intrigued for and was probably responsible for ensuring the succession of her son, Vasily III, the father of Ivan the Terrible.

G. Vernadsky, *Russia at the Dawn of the Modern Age* [Yale, 1959], pp. 22–6.

V. O. Klyuchevsky, *Course of Russian History* [Moscow, 1957], II, pp. 120–30.

J. L. I. Fennell, *Ivan the Great of Moscow* [London, 1961], pp. 315–24.

K. V. Bazilevich, *External policy of the Russian centralized State: Second half of the XVth century* [Moscow, 1952], pp. 83–8.

S. M. Solovyev, *History of Russia from Earliest Times* [Moscow, 1960], pp. 57–64.

Notes for Further Reading

THE most complete account of Ivan the Third and his period, available in English, is to be found in *Russia at the Dawn of the Modern Age*, by George Vernadsky, Professor Emiritus of Russian History in Yale University (Yale University Press, 1959). This is the fourth volume in the *History of Russia* which is being written by Professors George Vernadsky and Michael Karpovich. It contains an extensive bibliography of the relevant works in Russian and other languages.

The other indispensable monograph in English is *Ivan the Great of Moscow*, by J. L. I. Fennell which is an exhaustive study of Ivan III's foreign policy and diplomatic methods. It is possibly the most complete study of these aspects of Ivan III's reign in any language, but it is little concerned with economic or social developments. This, too, contains a valuable bibliography.

In Russian, references should be made to the three standard or "classic" histories which always repay study. They are N. M. Karamzin's *Istoriya gosudarstva rossiiskago*, S. M. Solovyev *Istoriya Rossii s drevneishikh vremen* and V. O. Kluyuchevsky *Kurs russkoy istorii*; the latest edition of the latter history has been published in eight volumes in Moscow, 1956–9.

Of the works of Soviet historians to which reference should be made, the most important are K. V. Bazilevich *Vneshnaya politika Russkogo tsentralizannogo gosudarstva. Vtoraya polovina XV veka* (Moscow, 1952) and L. V. Cherepnin *Obrazovanie Russkogo tsentralizannogo gosudarstva na Rusi v XIV–XV vekakh* (Moscow, 1960). The above and certain other Soviet historians have also published articles in *Istoricheskie Zapiska* and in *Voprosi Istorii* which should be studied.

Index

INDEX

INDEX

INDEX